Can The Human Being Thrive In The Work Place?

Dialogue As A Strategy Of Hope

Printed in the United States of America.
Grandville Printing Company
Grandville, Michigan

Published by:
Practice Field Publishing
100 Michigan Street NE
Grand Rapids, MI 49503
(616) 391-2017

Library of Congress Catalog Card
Number: 97-67675

ISBN: 0-9648264-3-7

<u>DEDICATION</u>

This book is dedicated to:

- Our families who sustain us with meaningful conversations of life.

- Our colleagues across the continent who willingly share the wisdom of their Souls and knowledge of their BodyMind.

- All those who are seeking ways to enrich their lives.

- Those who have experienced dialogue and are experimenting with it.

- Those who are searching and have not yet learned of its profound possibilities.

Prologue

This book emerges out of a desire to share the wisdom of hundreds of people who are using dialogue to enrich their lives in the work place. Since 1983 we have been uncovering ways to create empowered, healing health care environments. At the heart of this effort is the work of enhancing relationships between care providers, patients, and their families, as well as within our work teams. There is a growing Consortium of people from 40 health care settings across the United States and Canada who have come together to collectively share their experiences and learning about creating healthy work cultures. The Consortium is called the CPMRC Associate Consortium and it is connected through the CPM Resource Center (CPMRC). We at the CPMRC exist to enhance partnering relationships and world linkages for the generation of collective knowledge and wisdom that continually improve professional practice and community health care services. A list of the members of the ever growing Consortium can be found in the Appendix.

Our formal work in dialogue began about five years ago. It was a natural evolution because meaningful conversations are pivotal for healthy relationships and work cultures. It became apparent that we had to find practical ways to help strengthen the nature and depth of conversation in the work place. Dialogue provides that foundation.

The work of David Bohm and William Isaacs enhanced our learning. As we read more about dialogue, we began to encourage others to read and explore with us. We were challenged by those interested in deepening dialogue in their personal and professional lives.

We were very fortunate to establish a partnership with Beth Jandernoa and Glennifer Gillespie from Dialogos who have long been facilitators of bringing dialogue into work places and communities in the United States and South Africa. They shared their learning and experiences with us in a number of workshops over the years to follow. One of these workshops was conducted in conjunction with Judy Brown. Judy brings her learning and wisdom about dialogue to many companies and communities across the country. We also began to connect with others who were living dialogue and bringing it into the work place.

People around the world are using dialogue; there are groups, projects, and organizations forming to further the emergence of dialogue. One such initiative is led by William Isaacs. He leads the dialogue project at MIT's Organizational Learning Center which is part of the Sloan School of Management. This dialogue project has conducted action research experiments on dialogue and organizational learning around the world.

We introduced the principles of dialogue at the CPM National Conferences and offered hundreds of health care providers an opportunity to experience it, while simultaneously expanding our own dialogue skills. There was an extremely positive response from the Conference participants who were not used to exploring together and being together in this way. They welcomed the experience. We continued experimenting, learning, and growing in dialogue. Each experience provoked life changing learning and wisdom that is difficult to put into words.

Now dialogue is interwoven in all of our doing and being. Our work with Beth and Glennifer has expanded, and we are embarking on our first International Dialogue Conference for health care providers.

The intention of this book is to put our experience into words and offer a glimpse of the wisdom from the field generated from this work. Our hope is to unfold the essence of dialogue in our writing and bring it to life through the Wisdom From The Field stories. It is impossible to bring the full experience of dialogue through written word because each individual has his/her own unique experience. The experience is chosen by the participant through his/her ability to be open and engage in using the principles of dialogue either outwardly in the group and/or within self. So in acknowledging the fact that we cannot recreate the dialogue, we offer these excerpts that are merely a glimpse of the experience. We welcome you to join us in our journey with dialogue now and in the future.

Table of Contents
For The Journey

INTRODUCTION:
A journey using dialogue in the work place.

"It is something to paint a picture or to carve a statue and so to make a few objects beautiful. But it is far more glorious to carve and paint the atmosphere in which we work to affect the quality of the day. This is the highest of the arts."
- Henry David Thoreau

Welcome to a journey into the next millennium. Welcome back to those who began the journey with either the first or second book in the *Wisdom From The Field Series: A Journey From Old to New Thinking* (Wesorick, 1995) or *A Journey From Old to New Relationships in the Work Setting,* (Wesorick, 1996). This segment is about the use of dialogue as a strategy of hope for creating healthy work cultures. Dialogue connects people through respectful, open, honest communication around those things which matter most. It enhances continuous learning, expanded thinking,

and respectful relationships through meaningful conversation. Dialogue is about the nature of conversations that seek to learn, to recognize, to welcome, and to honor the expressions of wisdom that come from each individual. It is a strategy of hope because it helps one learn to live as a human being in today's work culture—where daily the Soul meets the external world.

For those just beginning this journey within the Wisdom From The Field Series, a repeat of some travel tips will be helpful:

- Please do not bring any baggage. We have found that it gets in the way, interferes with your desired pace, and prevents you from going to the most exciting places along the way.

- Stories will be shared throughout this series in order to capture the wisdom from the field. This wisdom will help guide us on this journey. It is shared to provoke your thinking and deepen your insights about relationships and dialogue.

- If you believe you see yourself or someone you know in a story, realize it may not be a story about any one individual. We will see ourselves and others because the stories are universal and represent reality across the practice field of life. The confidentiality of all individuals and practice settings is honored.

- The success of this journey rests with your thinking, your wisdom. Questions will be asked with that end in mind. That is also why the book is laid out with empty columns. These columns are placed for you to jot down your learning, thinking, questions, realizations, concerns, feelings and insights.

- We are not taking you on this journey; our intention is to partner with you. We will share our learning and assumptions as we travel, not for you to accept, but to help you examine, digest, and explore your thinking about dialogue and its impact on the quality of work cultures. You will be both comfortable and uncomfortable as you read. If you write in the margins "comfortable" or "uncomfortable" and what your thinking behind those feelings is, your personal wisdom will emerge. That is one of the goals of this book.

We believe this book will impact your life and the lives of everyone you touch. It

will expand on Book I which explored the shift of thinking about the essence of our work, and on Book II which concentrated on the principles of healthy relationships. The information is based on the wisdom from the field gathered from thousands of colleagues who have collectively come together to create work cultures that nourish the human being.

If we care about the health of this society, we must care about the work cultures. The quality of a person's life is influenced by the quality of the work culture. Many adults spend more waking hours at work than at home. When people leave the work place, mothers and fathers come home to their children, and they bring the impact, the nature, and the outcomes of their work culture through the front door with them. The milieu, thinking, and relationships that unfold in the work setting influence the milieu, thinking, and relationships in every home, thereby impacting the quality of life for all of society.

What is the importance of dialogue in the work place?

"To live in communion, in genuine dialogue with others is absolutely necessary if man is to remain human."
— Thomas Merton

*I*n what way have the conversations at work impacted the quality of your day? In what way have conversations strengthened or inhibited your relationships with others at work? We are human beings; that is, we are beings within a BodyMind. This being is often referred to as the Spirit, the Heart, or the Soul. We innately seek quality in our life which respects our personhood, our wholeness of BodyMindSpirit. In what ways have the conversations at work impacted your wholeness? What is the nature of those conversations that seem to energize you or drain you? The human being is apparently surviving every day in the work place. So what is the concern with it thriving? We believe it is a quality of life issue. Quality exists in the balance of an integrated BodyMindSpirit.

The human being cannot thrive if there is imbalance. The work setting influences the balance.

What are the patterns in the work setting that are impacting the balance of BodyMindSpirit? It is not necessary to quote the literature to prove that stress and chaos exist in the work setting. Those who work already know. It would be a waste of energy and time to look for someone to blame for the present nature of the work environment. Merton (1961) notes that blaming "turns a man to a fanatic, no longer capable of sustained contact with the truth, no longer capable of genuine love." That would not service the hopes for this book or improve the work culture.

What is the cause of stress in the work setting? Some think that the stress in today's work place is solely the result of the speed of change. However, the norm for a living creature is change. If the body does not change, it will die. If the work setting does not change, it will die. It is not the change or speed of change that is the problem. The stress comes from the person's response or perception of the change. This response is determined by the individual's *relationships*, first with self, and then with others. The nature of relationships not only plays a major role in the adaptability and impact of change in every work place, but also impacts the ability of each human being to thrive.

What is the nature of relationships in the work setting? Relationships in today's work settings are intimately linked to a history of hierarchy. Book II in the *Wisdom From The Field Series* looked closely at the old and new emerging patterns of relationships. See Table One on page 8 which provides a brief comparison of the Focus of Hierarchical Versus Partnering Relationships. Hierarchical or boss/subordinate relationships place value in the ability to produce and focus on getting things done and doing them as told. Hierarchy ignores the capacity of the Spirit, isolating a person in the narrow confines of "the power of another" or "the shadows of the tasks to be done." This type of relationship creates a disrespectful and dehumanizing work culture.

TABLE ONE

Comparison of the "Focus" of Hierarchical versus Partnering Relationships

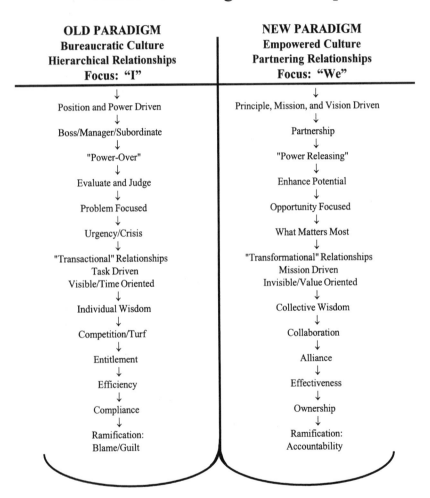

OLD PARADIGM Bureaucratic Culture Hierarchical Relationships Focus: "I"	NEW PARADIGM Empowered Culture Partnering Relationships Focus: "We"
↓	↓
Position and Power Driven	Principle, Mission, and Vision Driven
↓	↓
Boss/Manager/Subordinate	Partnership
↓	↓
"Power-Over"	"Power Releasing"
↓	↓
Evaluate and Judge	Enhance Potential
↓	↓
Problem Focused	Opportunity Focused
↓	↓
Urgency/Crisis	What Matters Most
↓	↓
"Transactional" Relationships Task Driven Visible/Time Oriented	"Transformational" Relationships Mission Driven Invisible/Value Oriented
↓	↓
Individual Wisdom	Collective Wisdom
↓	↓
Competition/Turf	Collaboration
↓	↓
Entitlement	Alliance
↓	↓
Efficiency	Effectiveness
↓	↓
Compliance	Ownership
↓	↓
Ramification: Blame/Guilt	Ramification: Accountability

Used with permission: © Wesorick, B. (1996) The Closing and Opening of a Millennium: A Journey From Old To New Relationships In The Work Setting. Michigan: Practice Field Publishing.

What is the nature of healthy relationships in the work place? Healthy relationships give wings to the Spirit and strong roots to the BodyMind. There will be no healthy work cultures unless there is a shift in the nature of relationships. There will be no shift in the nature of relationships without each person doing the work necessary to create healthy, partnering relationships. The work and the fundamental principles describing the nature of partnerships, or healthy relationships were explored in Book II of the series. See Table Two on pages 10-11 for a brief overview of the Principles of Partnership. The importance of the principles is echoed in a common request coming from the work field, "to be treated with respect and dignity." The Principles of Partnership describe what respect and dignity look like. The Wisdom From The Field starting on page 12 gives further insight into the impact of unhealthy relationships and the importance of meaningful conversation in the work place.

TABLE TWO

PRINCIPLES OF PARTNERSHIP

Principle of Intention: a personal choice to connect with another at a deeper level of humanness.

- Is not about doing, but becoming.
- Requires going within, so one can reach out.
- Connects at a place where purpose and meaning of life emerge.
- Connects with others, not to control, but to deepen insights into oneself and others.
- Requires vulnerability and starts with personal work of becoming a partner.

Principle of Mission: a call to live out something that matters or is meaningful.

- Centers around shared purpose, principles, and core beliefs—not position, policy/procedure, personal needs, bottom line, or power.
- Requires work of synchronizing personal and professional mission.
- Envisions work as an opportunity to make visible a person's purpose.

Principle of Equal Accountability: a relationship driven by ownership of mission, not power-over or fear.

- Holds each person to his/her choice: one is not the boss, one is not the subordinate.
- Knows competition and judgment interfere with individual and collective accountability to mission.
- Honors another's choice of role, responsibility and contribution.
- Is accountable to support others in achieving mission.
- Is not in relationship to evaluate or judge the other's work or worth.
- Knows credibility relates to quality of work, not type of work.
- Does not feed the ego, but nourishes the spirit.

Principle of Potential: an inherent capacity within oneself and others to continuously learn, grow and create.

- Sees self and others as continuous learners with untapped potential.
- Pursues clarity on others' roles and responsibility, not to judge but to integrate and potentiate one another.
- Taps others' expertise related to mission.
- Enhances choices, options, creativity and the imagination of others.

- Helps others recognize and tap personal wisdom.
- Seeks different perspectives but maintains common mission.
- Respects the individuality, uniqueness and diversity of self and others.
- Does not spend time molding others to be what he/she thinks they should be.
- Supports others as they evolve and change to achieve the mission.
- Explores self and others' assumptions to deepen wisdom.
- Knows when to ask for help.
- Requires compassion and ability to learn from and see beyond vulnerability.

Principle of Balance: a harmony of relationships with self and others necessary to achieve mission.

- Understands that personal stability deters being controlled by external forces.
- Accountable for personal balance, choice, and competency.
- Cares for self and others.
- Knows that harmony in work relationships, as the mission, is not optional.
- Addresses imbalance in work relationships.
- Helps others self-organize.
- Knows the source of energy is not in the tasks, but in the relationships.
- Works on continuous learning and shifting to improve relationships.

Principle of Trust: a sense of synchrony on important issues or things that matter.

- Starts with self, must trust self before trusting others.
- Knows personal trustworthiness precedes a trusting relationship with another.
- Recognizes that fear is a barrier to trust.
- Values the power that is within, not outside self.
- Does not have secrets, but shares information openly.
- Does not defend thinking, but shares it.
- Does not speak for the other, but seeks to hear the voice of the other.
- Does not try to get "buy-in" but dialogues to discover what is best for shared mission.
- Does not focus on who gets to make the decision, but what is the best decision.
- Does not blame, withdraw, instill guilt, rescue, fix, criticize or perpetrate.
- Focuses on quality of time together, not amount of time.

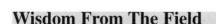

Wisdom From The Field

The group moved in the room hesitantly. The tension in the air was almost as palpable as a pulse. Kim sat down and stared ahead. Her jaw was tight, her lips tense, and her eyes filled with the readiness of a warrior. Jean sat in the chair, back slouched, looking at her lap. Chris sat and spoke about those who did not come. Karen seemed concerned and a bit apprehensive. Thelma came bouncing in, smiling and happy to be a part of "whatever this is about." Ken made a point of engaging most of them in social conversation. More peers joined them. They were all nurses and worked side by side with each other every day. Most had been working together over 5-10 years. They were very skilled in their work. They were coming to talk about the relationships in their department.

The principles of dialogue were used as the foundation for the conversation. The tension turned to expression, and the words were filled with a cry for help. The cry was not for better equipment, more educational opportunities, better hours, more vacation, or more money. It was for respect and dignity. They wondered how they had evolved to become as they were with each other. They went on to describe the competitiveness, the harsh judgment, how they complained about each other, and how "we eat our young." Chris said to Jean, "I have worked with you for 15 years and have no idea who you are. We are so busy doing, we don't take time to care, to really see each other and talk with one another."

As they shared their feelings, thoughts, and listened to each other, personal insights began to surface in the form of questions. Kim's question brought the group to silence when she asked, "I have wondered why we treat the patients with compassion and yet are so critical and disrespectful towards one another? We know it is important to care for patients, but not each other." Helen then commented, "I wonder why it is easier for me to be nice to someone (patient) with whom I will only be with for one hour, and so disrespectful to those I work with every day?"

As they talked, they became vulnerable with each other. They laughed, they cried, they listened, and they had meaningful con- versation which brought many realizations.

They had never been together like this before, they had never talked like this before. They decided they could no longer avoid or deny the work of relationships. What would they need to do to begin building a healing culture?

By using the principles of dialogue as the foundation for their conversation, something new and strange occurred, yet so familiar and filling to the Soul. Co-workers became whole people and as the web of interconnectedness grew and spread, healing occurred in the relationships. They did not have to be perfect nursing machines, they could be people.

What can be done to create a work place where the human being will thrive? Much has already been done to improve safety for the Body, as evidenced by present work conditions, policies, procedures, and safety standards. Much has been done in the work setting to improve the Mind, via continuous education, credentialing, certification, and expectation. What has been done to honor the Spirit, the core of our humanness? So often we hear people talk about the culture in the work setting. *Is the culture nothing more than the Spirit, the unseen presence of the Souls of*

the many who walk there daily?

Joseph Campbell (1988) stated, "The thing to do is learn to live in your period of history as a human being." What does that really mean? Does it mean that it is not enough to live, to eat, to work or simply survive? Is it a reminder to learn to experience the full capacity of being human, the capacity that exists within an integrated BodyMindSpirit? Is it a reminder to learn how to maintain the wholeness of our humanity so we might experience the joy of life--whether the period of history in which we live is one of cars or space ships, peace or war, downsizing or merging, etc.? Was Campbell suggesting we learn how to maintain our humanness in the face of whatever the reality appears to be in the rapidly changing world? If so, what would help us do that?

It is only through relationships that the Spirit of an individual is seen or known. It is only through healthy relationships that the Spirit thrives and finds joy. The importance of dialogue and the work of relationships was captured in the words of a nurse who said, "If we continue the way we are going, with no

meaningful conversation, no meaningful connection, we will perish." David Whyte (1994) notes that "Preserving the soul in corporate America means reclaiming all those human soul qualities sacrificed on the altar of organizational survival."

The fundamental connection, communication, and action necessary for new thinking and healthy relationships to flourish in the work culture is explored throughout this book. Dialogue addresses thinking, commun-icating and connecting with each other. It provides a fundamental approach to create cultures where relationships are cultivated with the same intensity as the physical tasks, the mental challenges, and the product creation. When the Spirit thrives, creativity and innovation thrive. Cultivating wholeness through relationships produces synergy that enhances every aspect of productivity. The importance of healthy relationships cannot be overstated--that is why Book II was written. However, thriving relationships cannot emerge without dialogue--that is the reason this book was written.

What is the call from the human being in the work place?

"We would like to be comfortable, we would like to be gratified, we would like not to be disturbed; but life, which is ever changing, ever new, is always disturbing to the old."
- *Krishnamurti*

Is the call simply for a healthy work culture? If so, what is a healthy work culture? Is it connecting with others in meaningful work? Is it a call to unleash the Spirit? Healthy work cultures versus unhealthy work cultures are no different from wellness versus illness. Dr. Dale Anderson (1995) in his book, *Act Now,* made a very important observation. He noted that the difference between **WELLNESS** versus **ILLNESS** is **We** and **I**. "We" is about connections, partnering relationships. Wellness is about relationships that connect one's being, one's personhood with another. Illness is about the status of the body. "I" focuses on the body. "I" can also stand for isolation. Without good relationships, without connections to the

human spirit of self or others, there is illness or unhealthy work cultures.

What is the nature of a thriving human being? In healthy relationships you connect with others in their humanness. It is not about doing, but about becoming or thriving. A closer look at the nature of the human *being* gives insights into the call from the work place. We all have had the opportunity to witness the *dramatic* expression of the human *being*. On TV we have seen video tapes showing people spontaneously acting to save the lives of others, even though they personally were in danger. We recognize and are moved by what is often referred to as "humane acts," acts in which one human being reaches out to another. The reaction within our mind may tell us that the action is dangerous, not thought out, or could have been done differently. The core of our humanity comes from a deeper place than the mind--it comes from within. It is here, on this level, that such acts make sense.

The human Spirit sits within. It is a place of compassion, love, energy, sensitivity, perseverance, hope, and forgiveness. When set free, the Spirit brings to the visible world behaviors that express all the invisible components of our humanity. When it is walled off or ignored the behaviors are not expressed. The following verse further describes the Spirit, "A Place Within."

A Place Within

Welcome to a place within
Where all the energy of being sits
No fear, No stress, No judgment
A place of compassion,
A place of forgiveness,
A place of transition.

It is steeped in silence
so to learn to listen.
It is steeped in silence
so to hear the voice of wisdom.
It is a place to dialogue
with the soul
and begin transition.

Welcome to a place within
where life is not events driven.
A place of passion and energy
for growth and personal transformation.

- Bonnie Wesorick

The Spirit always exists. It is like the sun, it is always there but it cannot be seen if blocked by the clouds or the earth. All living things connect at the Spirit level, the level of life itself. The Spirit reaches out and renews. Its capacity reaches far beyond the physical and mental boundaries of our BodyMind. Sometimes we see the Spirit more clearly because of the response of another. We feel it and know it through relationships with another. We can observe people's physical and mental abilities and never know their Spirit. If we lose our awe of the Spirit, we will lose our ability to treat others with respect and dignity.

Over time the invisible Spirit, which makes us uniquely human, can be ignored or overpowered. The work place is at risk for becoming an environment in which the Spirit is ignored. It can become a place where humans simply go to work, to perform, and to showcase physical and mental abilities. If the work place is only about performing or getting things done, individuals can focus on the task and disconnect from the Spirit. The eyes of the mind can become blind to the presence of the Spirit.

People can get things done and never acknowledge the real presence of another being. In fact, in the short run, by ignoring the Spirit, it appears more things can be done. Recognition of another is based on what is done, how fast, and how well. The more difficult, the more important the task, the more respect you deserve. It is not connecting with another at the being level, but at the doing level.

Over time, the unique human being can be discredited, overpowered, and overlooked. In the "doing" model, respect and dignity are something you work to get. Your worth must be proven. In the "being" model, respect and dignity are something you innately deserve. Campbell (1988) noted that "The head and heart should not be at war." When at war there is no personal balance. When the mind disconnects from the wisdom of the Spirit, there is no peace. The following Wisdom From The Field gives further insights into the importance of balance within BodyMindSpirit.

Wisdom From The Field

Mary was a nurse in the Intensive Care Unit. She was an excellent nurse. She loved her practice. Her work held great meaning

for her. She knew her competency, advanced skills, and caring made a difference in each person's life she touched. Suddenly Mary's life was instantly changed. She became seriously ill and was admitted to the very unit on which she practiced for years. She was diagnosed with post viral demyelinating syndrome leading to a quadriplegic state.

She faced an incomprehensible reality. She could do nothing for others or for herself. Her world crumbled, as did her identity and self esteem. Her worth, her self esteem, was embodied in what she could do. She thought, "I am what I do, I am what I produce. I cannot do anything, I am worth nothing." Mary thought she was worthy of respect and dignity because of what she could do, not because of who she was, a unique Spirit, a unique human being, now encased in a malfunctioning body.

Mary was unable to go inside and connect with her Spirit. Her broken body and her critical mind dominated her invisible Spirit. She needed help. The help she needed came from the relationships with her family, friends, and care providers. She stated, "I never could have done it alone. The unconditional love, caring, and comforting conversation of others reminded me I was more than my mind and body. I began to understand that I was a *human being*, not a *human doing*. The Spirit of others helped me reconnect to my Spirit and reminded me that this Spirit was created by God who loves me unconditionally for who I am, not what I produce." As Mary connected to her Sprit, the invisible place within, where the unique love, compassion, and energy of humanness sits, she was able to regain her self esteem and find peace.

Mary's story helps us learn about the Spirit, the place within. She noted that ironically, although chronically ill, she is healthier now than she was when her physical status was at its peak. She has balance. Her story reminds us to think about the millions of people who go to work every day and often are seen by others within the narrow confines of their job description or what they do, not who they are as a human being. Their humanness is narrowed to what they do—their personhood and wholeness ignored. Does this reinforce them to disconnect from their personhood as well?

Staying connected with self in wholeness first precedes being with others in wholeness. The words of Merton (1961) echoed concern when he said, "There is actually no more dangerous solitude than that of a man who is lost in a crowd, who does not know he is alone and who does not function as a person in a community either." He also noted that, "There are two things which men can do about the pain of disunion with other men. They can love or they can hate." Mary connected with her Spirit, her place within, a place of compassion and love. She did her own work. She made a choice. She first loved her self and then made a choice to connect with others in love.

When relationships are centered around doing, the interpersonal interactions are often of a judging nature; that is, one person is evaluating the effectiveness of another's actions. This is a process of dehumanization that separates or disconnects the Spirit from the BodyMind. Soon you are the "doing," not the "being" who is doing. In healthy relationships there is respect and dignity of the personhood as well as the performance.

Respect and dignity of the being calls for a human relationship that transcends doing.

The human being does not thrive by doing, but by becoming more deeply human. It is not the specific job, or the task that is important. It is the *intention* of the action. During a natural disaster, such as a flood, when people volunteer, it does not matter if one is the organizer of the relief plan, the person serving food, or the person cleaning the area for the now homeless families to live. Whether one helps during a flood, lets someone merge during heavy traffic, prays for disaster victims, picks up papers along side the road, sends money to a charity, respects each person at work, etc, all are demonstrating humanness. Dialogue helps us see that the intention of action, not the job or task at hand, is what leads us to becoming more human. Dialogue keeps the intention at the center of attention. The following dialogue speaks about intention.

Wisdom From The Field

During a dialogue session on relationships, the participants were sharing the characteristics of people with whom they had nourishing relationships. So often similar characteristics surface over and over. Common characteristics include trust, respect, honesty, caring, non-judgmental, good listeners, accepting, compassionate, sensitive, understanding, supportive, fair, and open. There is one characteristic that is usually mentioned, but rarely more than once, in any large group. It is "unconditional." When asked to elaborate one said, "It is unconditional acceptance." Another said, "It is unconditional love." One went on to share that, "We love others because we are part of them and they are a part of us—because we are human beings. It does not mean we have to like what they do. Because it is unconditional, it does not mean they have to earn our love or acceptance. We do not love them because we like them. We love them even when we do not like what they do, or their personality. It is the promise to care for them as a human being...it is hard. I am not sure what that would look like in the work setting. I am not sure if it is even possible, but I think it would make a difference, and we should aim for it."

The above thoughts about "unconditional love," parallel with Rachel Naomi Remen's

(1996) words: "Yet, all love is unconditional. Anything else is just approval." Approval connects others within the dimension of the mind, the judging of the doing. Intention connects with others beyond the task to a deeper place of compassion, the Soul.

What are the differences between a surviving and a thriving human being? Recently, a reporter asked why so much attention continues to be given to the sinking of the Titanic that occurred 85 years ago. He wondered why so many movies, books, and series have been created about this event. The response centered on the human drama that took place. Over 1,500 people went down with the ship, but over 700 survived. Because of the nature of this tragic event, there were numerous stories of humane acts. Humane acts are the visible expression of the core of our humanness. We are touched and interested in actions that reflect the essence of our humanity. We may even wonder how we would have responded. On the Titanic both types of human expression were present-- those connected to others at the Spirit level, a place of compassion, and those disconnected from the Spirit level. We are often compelled

by stories that unfold the nature of relationships where one being chooses to connect, and another chooses to disconnect. When we see compassion in another, it connects us to our own compassion, our own being. When we see a Spirit disconnected, it sometimes reminds us to think about what is most important.

We have noticed people surviving. We have seen human action in which the human spirit is not expressed. We have seen a person alive but disconnected from his/her Spirit. We have seen people come to work and do, and do, and do. We know the BodyMind can perform over and over again. We are surrounded by people doing this every day. Unfortunately the world seems to reward those who behave this way. Yet it comes with a price, a high price--dehumanization. We recognize robotic behavior as well as mental exhaustion.

Across this world there are many people punching in and punching out who are not expressing their being, or experiencing the connection with other beings. It has been said that the "Eyes are the window of the soul." Too often we see empty, glazed-over eyes, little connection, and no relationships—yet the work goes on.

We have also noticed people thriving. Thriving is good for the person and good for the work place. Few would deny the need for innovative thinking in the changing work setting. There can be no real change and no innovation without new, expanded thinking and healthy relationships. There can be no new and creative thinking without breaking old patterns and welcoming new thinking. The difficulty in the work setting is not new learning; it is the unlearning of old ways that interfere with discovery.

Beth Jandernoa (1995) describes dialogue as "An invitation to a safe place to begin to unfreeze the patterns of thinking in which we are stuck." Once the mind is freed from the meaningless rituals, routines, and patterns of thinking, it can connect and more easily recognize the wisdom of the Soul. In the process of unfreezing the thinking, the Spirit can be set free and its essence brought into the work place. The unique insights and energy of the Spirit can bring alternative approaches to the old patterns of judging, competition, and disrespect. The freedom of

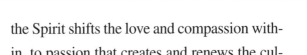

the Spirit shifts the love and compassion within, to passion that creates and renews the culture. The following verse speaks to the outcomes of a visible Spirit.

Connecting Our Beings

It is in the center of my being,
That I hear your unspoken words
Feel your inner spirit
Sense your hidden dreams.
It is in the center of my being
That your spirit and mine meet
so that we can co-create the world
One that reflects the reality of our souls
Transformed, visible.
A place where we no longer
Pretend that all is well
Ignore the crying of hearts
Or accept tolerance of control,
Power-over,
Fear or evil.
It is in the center of my being that
A place emerges where we can meet
To create a healthy work place
Where Body, Mind, and Spirit are one
So to experience the joy of our humanity.

- Bonnie Wesorick

Even though the old work and relationship patterns are not valued, there is hesitancy

to change them. The most common response to change is fear, a personal *stressor that comes from an overpowering mind.* Fear causes people to dig in their heels. Fear traps people in the moment, does not free them to live within the moment. Dialogue provides the fundamental tools to uncover fear and dissipate it. Kriegel, R. and Brandt, D., (1996) note that "Companies that make wholesale changes without addressing the complex system of thoughts, feelings, and wishes that constitute a human being are going to end up with a lot of heel dragging and silent sabotage." They also observed that "Management consultants who deal with companies in transition know the 'people' part of change is critical, and that it is most often overlooked and undervalued. The outcome of the change is determined by the people and their relationships with one another."

The need to thrive, not just survive can no longer be ignored. The human being is calling for a place where the Spirit is free to connect with the work at hand, to be present, recognized, and honored just as the BodyMind. Healing relationships, connections linked in wholeness, will then unfold and the human being will thrive.

In what way does dialogue enhance relationships in the work place?

"Relationship is a process of self-revelation, and without knowing oneself, the ways of one's own mind and heart, merely to establish an outward order, a system, a cunning formula has little meaning."
- Krishnamurti

*H*ealthy relationships do not just happen in the work setting or anywhere else. They evolve as the effort unfolds. Each person needs to begin with his/her own work. Dialogue facilitates this work because it promotes conversation that helps a person uncover personal thinking, not escape from it. Fox (1941) states, "It is the food which you furnish your mind that determines the whole character of your life. It is the thoughts you allow yourself to think, the subjects that you allow your mind to dwell upon, which make you and your surroundings what they are." Nothing changes without changes in thinking. Our patterns of thinking influence the relationships we have with each other. We can no longer ignore how each person's thinking connects to the quality of the work culture. Without conversation there will be no clarity of thinking and no healthy relationship.

Wisdom From The Field

A group was struggling with relationships between departments. One of the examples shared was as follows. "As soon as we come on our unit, we look to see what team is on the other unit. We know if it is Team A, we will have a good night. When Team B is on, we count on having problems." As the conversation unfolded, it became apparent that they had a good relationship with Team A, not Team B. They had little conversation with Team B. They realized they had disconnected from them. One described it by saying, "We tend to avoid talking with them or calling them wherever possible." The final realization was that they, themselves, were equally accountable for the actions of Team B; in fact, their behaviors enhanced just those things they did not like about Team B. They needed to dialogue with Team B, share their

thinking, and strengthen their relationships. Avoiding the issues, which was their pattern, did not help. In fact, this made it worse.

Instead of blaming Team B, the above group focused on themselves, uncovering their thinking and identifying inconsistencies. Krishnamurti (1992) noted, "Without understanding yourself, to seek a solution is utterly useless; it is merely an escape." Dialogue helps you know yourself and gives a sense of direction. The unit took action, but did not fall into the "quick fix." They started with dialogue and strengthened their own partnerships so they could connect with Team B.

We can no longer deny that we are connected to each other. We cannot avoid the work to strengthen the connections. The thought of being connected to others can be frightening. The verse, "Connecting Our Beings" on page 35 speaks to this fear. However, when we collectively connect at the Spirit level in the work setting, we are tapping into the endless energy and potential that comes from a connected humanity. Dialogue helps connect at the being level.

The Fear Of Connection

The spirit within
connects us all,
But the thought of that scares me.
Because, if it is so, I can
no longer blame you
For the things that trouble me so.

It could almost imply
that I am a part
of the things that annoy me the most.
It could almost imply
that I am the cause
of those things you do, that upset me.

To think that you are a reflection of me
causes distress I cannot bear.
I do not do the things that you do;
I do not say the things you say;
How could all of us be connected?

But if it is so, then what should I do
to change the things around me?
It calls me to change the world that I see
By changing not you, but what's inside me.

- Bonnie Wesorick

Ignoring the work of relationships or connections will further divide work teams and the tension will be felt by everyone. Since we co-create the world, we can stop the external constraints that crush our Spirit. Parker Palmer (1990) said, "It is easier to spend your life manipulating an institution than it is dealing with your own soul. It truly is. We make institutions sound complicated and hard and rigorous, but they are a piece of cake compared with our inner working." Dialogue helps us do our personal work and our relationship work. If we do not do our personal work, we will not have relationships with human beings, only human doings.

Dialogue is based on the assumption that every human, regardless of their age, sex, role, position, color, culture, credentialing, or status, has an innate wisdom that comes from the being within. Dialogue invites each person to go within and speak from that place. Although the Spirit is invisible, it is more powerful than the educated, disciplined mind or the perfect physique. However, the Spirit must be expressed and recognized. Dialogue provides the opportunity for a person to slow down, go within and bring forth his/her innate wisdom.

The place within is where indefinable love, passion, endless energy, forgiveness, sensitivity and compassion reside. The wisdom that flows from the place within is not necessarily based on life or work experiences, classroom knowledge, opinions or mental ability. Each human being is a hologram. In a hologram, the whole can be seen in each part. Each person brings another piece of his/her awareness that is different from any other persons, but in its expression, the whole of humanity is present. Dialogue is designed to deepen conversation so as to connect with another at the being level. Martin Buber describes dialogue as "A model of exchange among human beings in which there is true turning to another, and full appreciation of another, not as an object in a social function, but as a genuine being." Dialogue is a powerful way to communicate and demonstrate respect and dignity for another human being. It deepens conversations.

Dialogue helps people to be together in a different way. The principles of dialogue differ from the norms of hierarchical conversations. It is a slower pace and connects thinking rather than dividing, separating or analyzing it. William Isaacs (1993) notes that "Dialogue, the discipline of collective learning and inquiry, is a process for transforming the quality of conversation and the thinking that lies beneath it." He states, "Dialogue can be defined as a sustained collective inquiry into the processes, assumptions and certainties that structure everyday experience." Dialogue is based on hope, hope that comes from the realization that collective insights far exceed individual insights. Through collective insights, new knowledge emerges.

Dialogue is an outward invitation to connect in more meaningful conversation. It provides an opportunity to know the human being. Thomas Merton (1961) eloquently described the outcomes of living without dialogue when he said, "But to live in the midst of others, sharing nothing with them but the common noise and the general distraction, isolates a man in the worst way, separates him from reality in a way that is almost painless. It divides him off and separates him from other men and from his true self." He describes the absence of Soul. When our work does not connect with the knowing inside, it eats away at the expression of our humanness. Dialogue is an attempt to relate beyond the general noise and distractions of the rituals, routines, and patterns of daily tasks.

Conversations in many work settings would rarely be classified as dialogue. The usual communication patterns develop out of a need to get things done and are often based on hierarchical relationships. Hierarchical conversations evolve around information rendering, telling someone what to do, how to do it, and letting them know if they are doing it well enough. In hierarchy, communication is seen as an opportunity to defend one's point of view or opinions, win over, judge or get "buy-in" from others.

Just as there is a call by this society for a paradigm shift from hierarchy to partnering relationships, so is there a call to live the principles of dialogue: the foundation for respectful and dignified conversations that honor the personhood of another. The principles of partnership parallel with the principles of dialogue. The principles of dialogue are briefly defined in Table Three on page 40. Each will be explored throughout this text.

TABLE THREE

PRINCIPLES OF DIALOGUE

Intention: The willingness to create a safe place to learn collectively, to share thinking, listen to the thinking of another, be surprised, and honor the presence of BodyMindSpirit.

Listening: The willingness to learn to listen to self and others with the BodyMindSpirit—without judgment and competition.

Advocacy: The willingness to share personal thinking, and what is behind the thinking, with the intention of exposing, not defending it.

Inquiry: The willingness to ask questions that dig deeper and uncover insights and new learning.

Silence: The willingness to experience and learn by reflecting and discovering the lessons from personal awareness, words unspoken, or the quiet of the Soul.

Dialogue helps to cultivate and live the principles of partnership because dialogue and partnership connect at the same place, the Soul. It does this by inviting others together in such a way that it strengthens the ability for each person to live the principles of partnership. The work over the last 14 years to create partnering cultures in health care settings across the country has been a challenge. *The introduction of dialogue has strengthened the shift more than any other effort.* It is that realization which drove this book. See Table Four on page 42 which gives a brief overview of how dialogue helps partnership emerge. In addition, each of the following chapters will explore how the principles of dialogue enhance partnership.

TABLE FOUR

Dialogue Helps Create Cultures Of Partnerships

PRINCIPLES OF PARTNERSHIP		HOW DIALOGUE STRENGTHENS PARTNERSHIPS
Intention: A personal choice to connect with another at a deeper level of humanness.	⇒	Extends an invitation to connect with another in a respectful conversation which honors the Body-MindSpirit.
Mission: A call to live out something that matters or is meaningful.	⇒	Provides an opportunity to speak about, and together with others, dig deeper into those things that matter or are meaningful to each person.
Equal Accountability: A relationship driven by ownership of mission, not power-over or fear.	⇒	Creates a practice field where there is no position, role, hierarchy, judgment or competition. There is equal accountability to listen, inquire, share, and learn.
Potential: An inherent capacity within oneself and others to continually learn, grow, and create.	⇒	Provides a renewal process that honors the right of each person to speak from his/her personal wisdom. It ponders the mystery of another. It teaches others through advocacy, listening, and inquiry to tap into, and dig deeper into personal and collective wisdom. It connects diversity which unleashes and creates new thinking, uncovers new possibilities, opens new doors and unfolds new alternatives for choices.
Balance: A harmony of relationship with self and others necessary to achieve mission.	⇒	Welcomes silence which helps individuals listen to themselves, others, and then reflect. It exposes inconsistencies. It brings awareness of personal thinking which uncovers deep values--important for self balance. Personal independence precedes healthy interdependence. It helps find common understanding and creates a passion to connect in common purpose.
Trust: A sense of synchrony on important issues and things that matter.	⇒	Uncovers the truths that dissipate fear. The practice field creates a safe, respectable place that helps uncover and expose basic thinking. There is no attempt to guess or judge. It honors diversity and seeks to connect patterns. It is easier to listen to someone's voice when one's own voice is heard. Inquiry helps break patterns of assumptions and checks into deeper meanings. Deeper, yet personal thinking seems to mirror universal truths which connect beings.

PRINCIPLE OF DIALOGUE: INTENTION
How does the intention of dialogue transform conversation and relationships?

"Without linguistic honor there can be no community, there can be no ethic, there can be no love, there can be no creative vision, there can be no peace, and there can be no relationship."
- Paula Gunn Allen

*T*he nature of conversation and communication helps people in the work setting connect in a different way and to form new relationships. The principle of intention is a willingness to establish new ways to deepen communication and conversation. It is a willingness to create a safe place to learn collectively, to share thinking, to listen to the thinking of another, to be surprised, and to honor the wisdom and presence of BodyMindSpirit.

The dehumanization of the work setting is often evident in the conversations that are

being conducted. Conversations provide insights into the meaning and purpose of work and the relationships necessary to carry out the work. Have you heard any of the following? "I have never been busier, working harder, been less informed, and further behind." "The stress is growing each day." "No matter how much you do, someone is expecting it to be done faster and with fewer resources." "The pressure is increasing every day." "No one seems to care about people; they only care about getting things done." "What really matters around here is the bottom line." "The only thing that matters here is the number of FTE's (full time equivalents), the speed with which they complete their tasks, or their productivity." Have you ever heard someone say, "I just put my time in at work, so I can get home and do what I love?" Superficial conversations produce superficial relationships. Meaningful conversations produce meaningful relationships.

In what way does conversation link human *beings*? Conversations that seek to connect with another are very different from conversations built around control or getting things done. Conversations that center on getting things done focus on the task at hand, who will do it, when to do it, and whether it was done well. Conversations that center around control focus on defending one's point of view, winning, judging or getting "buy-in." Conversations to connect evolve around learning, exploring and uncovering with another. Conversations that help the human *being thrive* are intentionally carried out with respect for the core of humanness. It is not the length of the conversation, it is the intention to recognize and respect the wholeness of another. When conversations come from the Soul, the sacredness of the words are realized. The following Wisdom From The Field draws attention to the impact of conversation.

Wisdom From The Field

Barbee and Troy had been trying for almost three years to have a child. They longed to share their love with a child. They were plagued with infertility problems. They had decided to do whatever they could to make their dream a reality. Barbee began with the usual fertility drugs and then proceeded to more advanced approaches including multiple artificial inseminations, in vitro, and surgical fertilization. Their life became an emotional roller coaster; one day hopes were high, another day was filled with the disappointment of a failed treatment. Barbee searched to find meaning in this difficult time. She especially struggled after she finally became pregnant, only to learn the child was forming in her fallopian tube and she would have to have it removed. She valued the support and comfort of others. She stated that the events impacted "The whole fabric of my life. I was sad with each loss and very vulnerable."

She noted that during times of difficulty and sadness, she became very aware of the words of others. She was needing comfort. At times she found the words of others insensitive, even dehumanizing. She was especially hurt by the flip response of some health care providers. It was not that they did not do the right things to her physically when she was hospitalized, but their words were about what they were doing to her, with no acknowledgment of her grief. There was no attempt to connect with her personally. They cared for her body, not her Soul. She gave the following example of what people said, "Another tubal pregnancy; we will have you in and out in a hurry." There was no acknowledgment of her loss and grief--another way to devalue it. "You should be glad, the baby was probably not healthy." "Next time it will be twins." "Just keep trying." They did not know her story or they would have known that she could not afford to keep trying.

A fellow colleague at work said, "Children are a big problem, cause a lot of stress, and don't behave; you should be glad you don't have children." Barbee talked of the many who did not acknowledge her loss--just ignored it. "They probably did not know what to say," she thought. She understood they could not fix the situation, but there was no connection, no compassion or respect for her personhood in their silence, words, or actions.

In what way would the communication have been different if there was intention to connect with Barbee? Conversation can be superficial and dehumanizing. The intention to connect is the antidote for dehumanization.

Paula Gunn Allen reminds us "That you should, in your being, recognize that when you speak, your utterance has consequences inwardly and outwardly and that you are accountable for these consequences." Dialogue teaches us the power of words and linguistic honor. Dialogue is conversation that synchronizes the knowledge of the Mind with the awareness of the Soul. It humanizes conversation. It teaches us about the sacredness of our words.

In dialogue, there is intention to link participants one to another in deeper ways because there is no agenda, no hierarchy, no judgment, no task to be done. It is about deep listening as much as it is about speaking. It is about genuine inquiry into ways of thinking so to explore, reflect, listen, and examine personal thinking as well as another's way of thinking. It is based on the willingness of each person to examine his/her own thinking and be influenced by the thinking of others. Being human is not a hierarchical issue, it is something we all have in common. It is not about doing a task, but about becoming even more human. Becoming more human does require action and the action requires energy. The source of endless energy sits in the center of our being. Dialogue taps that energy.

Dialogue is a desire to be genuinely surprised and experience the "ah ha" of new learning. It is a discipline that leads to insights and actions that have positive long term outcomes. When old ways of thinking are broken, the innovation and creativity that comes from the whole being is given the opportunity to be expressed. Dialogue leads to different outcomes or it leads to what Jones (1995) would describe as giving "Tangible form to some aspect of the unformed potential that has its roots in the invisible world." It creates new cultures.

Dialogue draws attention to the whole by connecting diverse individual learning with collective insights. Dialogue reveals inconsistencies, contradictions, and inadequacies of old thinking patterns and assumptions. It is a human to human interaction, a relationship not based on doing, but based on the thinking that underpins becoming. It strengthens the fundamental skills necessary for conversations which leads to expanded thinking and relationships. The intent of dialogue is to

create conversation that helps the human being thrive. It is a powerful way to connect with another in the moment, not to be lost or trapped in just the activity of the moment.

PRINCIPLE OF DIALOGUE: LISTENING
What helps one listen to the human being?

"Real communication can only take place where there is silence."
- Krishnamurti

*T*here can be no dialogue without listening. Listening is harder than it seems, partially because it is so much more than being quiet or not speaking. It is the ability to engage or synchronize the personhood of one being with the personhood of another. It is much more than just hearing the words. It is about being present and welcoming the voice of another.

Bohm (1989) spoke of the outcome of dialogue as being similar to "A stream of meaning flowing among and through us and between us." It is a process that facilitates the immersion of oneself into the waters of collective thinking and learning. It provides the opportunity to think and learn with self

and others. It uncovers the unique capacity that exists in every person to teach and learn. Bohm noted it exposes and alters the "tacit infrastructure" of thought, which leads the participants to a collective discovery and alignment, not forced agreement or compliance. Therefore, dialogue requires deep listening to self and others.

Listening begins with the individual. Before you can listen to another, you need to listen to yourself. Dialogue teaches you to listen to yourself. What are your patterns of listening? Do you listen more with your body, your mind, or your soul? The mind can distract from deep listening because it tends to judge. The result is competitive or defensive listening. For example, when someone is speaking to you, do you find yourself preparing a response to what they are saying? Or is your first response to determine whether or not their words are credible? Do you find yourself judging their personal style? During these times you are distracted from the kind of listening that dialogue hopes to achieve. Listening is an expression of deep respect and acceptance of another.

Deep listening is not for the purpose of judging or trying to fix something. It is to deepen your thinking and learning. It requires a personal effort to be aware of your own listening style so you can contribute and participate. For example, what do you do when you are comfortable or uncomfortable with what is being said? These feelings are cues for you to ask yourself, "Why am I comfortable or uncomfortable?" Am I uncomfortable because the speaker is pushing against my assumptions, using words that push my buttons, or am I unclear about what is being said? Asking these questions of yourself helps you uncover your thinking. Inquiry is a willingness to ask questions that dig deeper into your own thinking and other's thinking. Self questions prevent you from making assumptions that the words used by the speaker mean the same thing to him/her as they do to you. Dialogue is a respectful conversation where assumptions are checked-out.

Knowing why you are comfortable with something that a person is saying is equally as important as knowing why you are uncomfortable. It is important because sometimes the things that you are the most

comfortable with are your greatest barriers to expanding your thinking. When you ask yourself questions about your comfort or discomfort you are becoming clearer, and that will not only help you, but also the group. By the way, sometimes what you uncover is that you have no idea why you think one way or the other...you never really thought about it. That is great learning! That is the gift of listening to yourself. See Table Five for the Introspection Tool which can be used as you listen to others speak, or as you read another's words.

Deep listening calls for a conscious decision to listen differently, not to judge, prove, or compete. It takes practice because it calls for quieting and clearing of your own mind. In what way do you listen in the following situations: if you know or do not know the person; if you like or do not like the person; if you trust or do not trust the person. Deep listening teaches you to let go of your patterns. It helps you side step your personal bias. It does not call for you to give up your thinking. It calls for you to "suspend" your thinking and listen from within, the place of quiet, acceptance, sensitivity, compassion, love, and forgiveness.

TABLE FIVE

SHIFTING INTO DIALOGUE
INTROSPECTION TOOL and PERSONAL WORKSHEET

DEFINITIONS:

Intention: The willingness to create a safe place to learn collectively, to share thinking, listen to the thinking of another, be surprised, and honor the presence of BodyMindSpirit.

Listening: The willingness to learn to listen to self and others with the BodyMindSpirit--without judgment and competition.

Advocacy: The willingness to share personal thinking, and what is behind the thinking, with the intention of exposing, not defending it.

Inquiry: The willingness to ask questions that dig deeper and uncover new insights and new learning.

Silence: The willingness to experience and learn by reflecting and discovering the lessons from personal awareness, words unspoken, or the quiet of the soul.

Comfortable	Uncomfortable*	Inquiry: Questions that will Expand my Understanding	Patterns of Thinking/ Behavior	My Key Learning

*TIP: When you feel uncomfortable with the speaker's perspective, these questions may enhance your learning:
- Is the speaker's perspective pushing against my assumptions?
- Am I unclear on the speaker's underlying thinking?
- Is my thinking about this issue fragmented, competitive, reactive?

The following verse reflects one person's struggle to practice listening.

My Gift

We gather in a circle.
He begins to speak.
It takes great energy to listen at first.
My Body feels gnarled, tight, unsatisfied,
Worried about appearance and position within
the circle; clouds surround my ears.
Rising out of a sense of politeness,
my focus returns to his words.
What did he say?

Not knowing if his phrases are pleasing,
I continue to focus.
Discomfort causes my Mind to awake;
it clatters and babbles.
My existence within this circle
turns to critique.
He continues to speak
but I can only hear myself.
I watch his lips move as my Mind taunts me
into a superior position.
I respond within, to my Mind's voice, without
utterance of my personal thinking.
What did he say?

Holding my attention most is when
she speaks familiarity.
Justification of my thoughts
creates a strong bond.

Comfort causes my Mind and Body to awaken;
it nods acceptance.
I begin to question this bond
my Mind has created.
Could this bond simply represent bondage to
those things I know best?
If so, then what have I learned from
the words she has spoken?
What did she say?

So I speak within this circle,
sharing quandaries from within.
He responds with a question.
She deepens the meaning of my words
with her wisdom.
Reflecting on my thinking, silence falls
around me and I am still.
Shh, What do I hear coming from
this peaceful moment?
Spirit's door has been opened,
new awareness is here.
To have listened is my gift.
I feel alive.

- Diane Hanson

When you only listen with your mind, it is natural to judge what the other is saying. A judging mind listens very differently from an accepting Soul. The mind is busy preparing a counter to the words spoken, often noticed by the opening statement, "but." The soul frees you from judgment, stress, and competition, which then frees you from defending your views or judging another's. It is in that freedom, which comes from letting go, that leads to true exploration and uncovering of the thinking behind the thinking. Listening opens the door to experience the other principles of dialogue, inquiry and advocacy, which deepen the conversation. In addition, once you become connected to your Soul, it is an invitation for everyone else to speak from their Souls as well. When there is freedom of BodyMindSpirit, expression, creativity, and new knowledge emerge.

Listening in dialogue is not listening for the purpose of fixing something or finding a solution. In our meetings we often listen so we can resolve an issue, and that is a different type of listening. It is listening for answers, or predetermined outcomes. In dialogue we are listening for discovery. When we listen for answers, we miss the potential, and the unexpected. Once we demand an answer, or think we know, or have found the answer, then we must defend it, and we can no longer listen in the same way.

Listening to make a decision is very different from listening to learn. Dialogue is not about making decisions, it is about exploring. It calls for a different set of skills and different processes. William Isaacs, in *The Fifth Discipline Fieldbook* by Senge, Roberts, Ross, Smith, and Kleiner (1994), differentiates by noting that "In skillful discussion, you make a choice; in a dialogue, you discover the nature of choice." Listening helps one learn how to handle polarization and connect diverse thinking so to increase alternatives, which is an integral part of a successful process of informed choice.

Because dialogue is a slower pace, it allows for reflection. Deep listening engages the BodyMindSpirit and helps one become equally aware of what is said, and what is not said. Reflection is a time to listen to the wisdom from within. Vaclav Havel, President of Czechoslovakia, (1990) spoke of the necessity of reflection when he said, "The salvation of this human world lies nowhere else than in the human heart, in the human power to reflect, in human meekness, and in human responsibility." Dialogue invites reflection. It is in reflection of the

quiet listening of dialogue that the heart can be heard as shown in the following Wisdom From The Field.

Wisdom From The Field

Paula Underwood (1996) spoke of the many learnings about listening that she received from her father. He was helping her learn to become the history keeper for her Iroquois lineage. Over and over again, he helped her learn to listen closely to what people said, asking her to repeat back what she had heard. One day, following another conversation between her father and their neighbor, Mr. Thompson, he asked her what Mr. Thompson had said. When she gave back Mr. Thompson's story verbatim he said, "OK, that's pretty good, but did you hear his heart?" She was young enough that she thought he meant listening to the heartbeat of those around her, but she learned that he meant hearing the heart behind the words. Finally she learned to hear the heart behind Mr. Thompson's stories. "He tells you the same stories again and again because he's asking you to keep him company in his memories. He is lonely and asks you to join him." "Ummm, you have learned to hear his heart," her father replied.

Have you ever been talking to someone, but they were not listening? What was that like? Did you notice it was more difficult for you to speak? Did it become harder to find what you thought were the right, most accurate words? How different is it when you are speaking and the person is listening intently? Do you recall how that impacted you? Did you find that as he/she listened closely, it made it easier to speak, especially from your heart? Listening honors the personhood. It renders respect which empowers the speaker.

The following quotes represent the key learning shared by participants following an open dialogue:

- "The sense of hearing is something we take for granted. The gift of listening needs to be fostered, nurtured, and exercised to receive the full potential. The art of dialogue is communication that should be utilized to help promote peace and understanding into the new millennium."

- "Listening is an acquired skill, not an innate one."

- "Disinterested listening is demeaning to the speaker and harms relationships."

- "Focused listening is a skill that needs to be developed, actively involves both the sender and receiver."

- "It is so important to listen for what we cannot hear."

- "It's not speaking that makes the difference, it is my listening. I am struck by the impact of listening on the speaker as well as the listener!"

- "The power of listening—how really hearing others leads to knowing/learning about oneself."

- "How we listen can be a key factor in what is heard and what is being said."

Deep listening leads to spontaneous silence. It is in silence that the spoken and unspoken voices can be truly heard. Nouwen (1981) says, "Silence reveals itself as the mystery of the future world by teaching us to speak. A word with power is a word that comes out of silence. A word that bears fruit is a word that emerges from the silence and returns to it." It is the wisdom that comes from the collective synchrony of BodyMindSoul connection. Listening and silence go hand in hand. Chapter IX, Principle of Dialogue: Silence; beginning on page 92, will delve deeper into the concept of silence. The Wisdom From The Field below gives further insights.

Wisdom From The Field

Each year the CPM Resource Center holds a National Conference to bring together people from across the continent to collectively learn how to improve our mission to positively influence the health of this society and improve the relationships necessary to make that happen. Each year we ask some of the people for whom we are privileged to care to come and help us grow. We ask them to share their realizations about the impact of our service on their health. We asked children who had received care and their families to be with us. One of the teenagers was so excited. He wondered if the people would ask questions of him. It would be so much fun to have people ask him questions, like reporters do of athletes during press conferences. During the preparation he remarked more than once how he

looked forward to the question period after the panel had spoken. We assured him, based on the patterns in the past, that he would be asked questions. We had no idea what was going to happen.

We believe the response to the panel was influenced by the Conference theme of dialogue. The principles of dialogue were explored and reinforced throughout the three days. During the afternoon, which preceded the panel presentation, over 700 participants broke into multiple small groups to experience dialogue. Following the two hour dialogue sessions the group came together to hear the panel.

It was apparent that the principles of dialogue were being lived in the convention hall. Although the room was large, when the children and their families spoke, you could feel the quiet of listening. It was hard to believe the stillness of hundreds. The panel, initially a little tense, began to relax and the nature of their sharing seemed comfortable and deep. They shared their thinking and feelings about the impact of our care on their lives. They shared from a vulnerable, wise place. Each spoke from his/her heart.

Following the panel's sharing, the session was open for questions. However, no one spoke. No one even made an attempt to go to the open microphones spaced throughout the convention hall. We waited and there was silence. It was the silence of awe. It was the silence of reflection on the wisdom spoken from the children and their parents. It was respectful. It was a surprise. It made sense. Even the teen who was so eager to be asked questions understood. In the silence he could hear the unspoken questions. See the verse, "Listen, Be Still," below.

Listen: Be Still

Listen, Be Still. It is in stillness
that we hear the Spirit Teacher.
Listen, Be Still. It is in silence
that we hear the voice
of inner wisdom.
Listen, Be Still. Go Within.
It is within that we learn
to heal self and others.
Listen, be still . . . listen, be still.

- Bonnie Wesorick

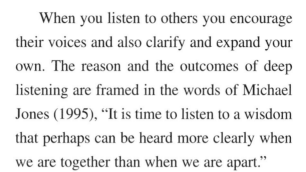

When you listen to others you encourage their voices and also clarify and expand your own. The reason and the outcomes of deep listening are framed in the words of Michael Jones (1995), "It is time to listen to a wisdom that perhaps can be heard more clearly when we are together than when we are apart."

PRINCIPLE OF DIALOGUE:
ADVOCACY
Do we have less capacity when one voice does not speak?

"This I believe, is the great western truth: That each of us is a completely unique creature and that, if we are ever to give any gift to the world, it will have to come out of our own experience and fulfillment of our own potentialities, not someone else's."
- Joseph Campbell

$\mathcal{D}$ialogue helps create bridges from one thought to another...and soon the glimpse of the whole can surface. For this to occur, the principle of advocacy is needed. In dialogue, advocacy is the willingness to share personal thinking, but without defending it. It calls for a person to be vulnerable enough to share personal assumptions, feelings, and the thinking behind the thinking and feelings. It calls for a person to speak from "I," but the "I" of wholeness.

Advocacy in dialogue is not about proving your expertise. It is a different way of sharing your knowledge, thinking, or feeling.

It takes away the usual hierarchical pressure to prove a point or provide an answer. It is not about answers, but more an invitation to explore. During advocacy you share your thinking and then invite others to take it deeper. This is done by saying, "These are my thoughts, how are they similar or different from yours? Does my thinking stimulate any realizations for you? What questions does my thinking invoke in you?"

Advocacy shows a willingness to be vulnerable enough to share your own thinking and what lies behind your thinking. It is the willingness to go deeper than the words of the Body and Mind and bring words from the Soul. This sharing is not for the purpose of convincing or defending. It is not about scripted thinking, but spontaneous sharing. Advocacy allows you to see yourself. It is fundamental to a positive relationship with another. It helps you know yourself better. It is also a way of honoring yourself, your thinking, and feelings as shown in the following wisdom.

Wisdom From The Field

Following a dialogue that was focused on the desire to shift the present strong hierarchical culture to one of partnerships, each person responded to the question, "What change in myself would help to create a partnering culture in our work setting?" During the dialogue a common theme emerged within the group of not feeling valued by administration or each other. As they spoke, people would give examples of situations in which they felt their work, their effort, their feelings, their personhood were not valued. There was no feeling of support. A common comment was that "no one offered to help," or "no one acknowledged their situation, and in fact, did things to worsen it." As they talked about not being valued, they would give examples of situations in which they felt others were insensitive.

As each person spoke to what change they would make in themselves, an interesting pattern emerged. There were many who spoke about the need for them to get out of the victim stance and have the courage to speak up. The change they would make was to ask for help when it was not offered, to share what they were thinking, and to address the issues that gave them a sense of being devalued, not just keep them bundled up inside and have them eat away at their spirit.

There was a realization of the importance of speaking up, the importance of advocacy. One nurse shared that "It would take great courage for me to do that. The reason I believed it was so hard was that, when I was in nursing school, I was told not to speak up, not to complain, but just do the work the best I could. That is what good nurses do."

Advocacy is not about complaining. Quite the contrary. It is about bringing personal thinking and feeling into a situation so to avoid being a victim. It is a way to help others who are listening avoid being perpetrators or rescuers. It comes from a place of trust, not fear.

The principle of advocacy is very different from hierarchical conversations based on control, manipulation, "power-over," judging or defending. It is personal thinking brought to the group for the sake of adding one more piece of wood to the fire of learning. It does not dictate the size of the fire. It is a small, but completing perspective similar to adding a small piece to a universe size puzzle. Advocacy calls for each of us to bring our voice, our own unique voice, to the table. It can be done in any place, in many different ways. Once released into the world, it expands forever.

Judy Brown (1996), in her book, *The Choice*, talks about her father's choice to end his life with the help of Dr. Kevorkian. It is a beautiful example of advocacy. She is willing to expose her thinking about a very controversial subject. She is willing to share the thinking behind her thinking. She clearly speaks from her BodyMindSpirit. The power of her words are the result of the transparency of her Soul. She is not speaking to convince any of us that assisted suicide in terminal illness is for us, or anyone else. She is speaking so that each of us might uncover our own thinking. She eloquently challenges the reader to go deeper without a hint of manipulation, judgment or defensiveness.

Judy teaches the principles of dialogue to people across this country in her consulting practice. These principles come alive in this very personal book. Regardless of how you feel about assisted suicide, you will have deepened your understanding of this

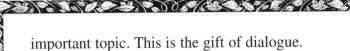

important topic. This is the gift of dialogue.

Advocacy honors diversity which is a requisite for meaningful dialogue. At the beginning of dialogue we often notice who is present and consider whose diverse voice is missing. Diversity pushes against the known and exposes different thinking while uncovering new connections and new possibilities. It strengthens the road to common ground on those things which matter most. Common ground does not require homogeneity or preclude diversity. Without diversity, we cannot fully know what matters most to us. We simply accept what we presently understand or think. Diversity of thinking expands insights and offers new choices. *It creates connectiveness without dominance.*

Dialogue connects the Mind and Soul resulting in the emergence of different choices. The choices are not limited by "what should be," or "what is expected." They come from freedom, not control. At times it seems we think our purpose is to control the thinking and the things around us, even the earth. It is easy to forget what is gained when we live with the intention to create a haven on this earth for the expression of each person's Spirit. Living the principles of dialogue helps create a culture that becomes a haven for the release of each Spirit's unique purpose and wisdom which enhances the whole living universe.

When diversity is seen as conflict, it prevents growth. Dialogue provides conditions that teach us to welcome diversity and not see it as conflict. It provides for us an opportunity to see the other side of conflict. It teaches us to go deeper beyond the construction of the Mind and connect it with the eyes, ears, understanding and courage of the Soul which brings a different kind of learning.

Phyllis Kritek (1996) described the desired outcomes of dialogue in times of conflict when she said, "I have learned to value these conflicts, however, because they have called forth in me a commitment to courage, self-honesty, and learning that I might not have acquired without the conflict. They have sometimes fatigued me but have not permitted me to indulge in prolonged periods of sloth. They have stretched and thus enriched me—even the ones that enraged or frustrated me the most. And they

have given me opportunities for personal growth and fulfillment that I might not have known had I lived in a more naturally harmonious set of givens." Her eloquent words speak to the personal transitions possible when dialogue continues in the face of extreme diversity.

It is only through the richness of diversity that the patterns of universal principles or truths can be revealed. Diversity teaches us that often differences are a part of the same truths. There would be no light if there was no darkness, no white if there was no black, and no day if there was no night. Diversity offers an opportunity for a deeper awareness which provides a momentum for the generation of new knowledge. Dialogue does not just honor diversity, it celebrates it. It links diversity and deepens the roots of knowing. Advocacy gives voice to diversity and makes music. It is beautiful music—music from the piano of life where both hands are in synch, but each doing different things.

The nature of dialogue helps us not only to learn to be comfortable with ambiguity, uncertainty and change, but also to welcome it and seek it out so to learn and grow more.

When we stop defending our views, or what we think things are or should be, we are freed to uncover new thinking and new learning. A personal outcome of advocacy is to know oneself better. A collective outcome is the uncovering of truths, and the exposure to new knowledge. Each contribution plants a seed that will grow beyond the moment. What a respectful way to help the human being thrive. When you become comfortable with the principle of advocacy, you are learning to bring your Soul into the work setting.

PRINCIPLE OF DIALOGUE: INQUIRY
In what way do questions hold the power to unlock new insights?

"Questions are an invitation to join once again in the endless and enduring cycles of creation, cycles that are always incomplete and unfinished because there is always more to come."
- Michael Jones

*H*ave you noticed behaviors in others that did not match what they said they supported or believed? Have you been in a meeting where an impasse was encountered within a group around an issue that initially seemed small, but grew out of proportion? Have you problem solved issues only to have them resurface over and over again? In your culture, are questions welcome, or are they seen as a disruption and disagreement? The presence of such experiences are symptoms calling for a deeper level of inquiry. They are telling us our discussions and decisions may be words that are swirling at the surface of deeper issues. How can we get to these deeper issues?

In many organizational cultures we are still novices at the art of using questions to continually uncover new learning and insights. When we were children, asking questions was our way of learning and evolving our thinking. In its purest form, inquiry offered us excitement, fun, and learning. Somehow, we have lost sight of this as an important method of exploration and growth. William Isaacs, in the *Fifth Discipline Field Book* by Senge et al. (1994), tells us inquiry comes from a Latin word meaning "to seek within," whereas the Latin word for decision literally means "to murder alternatives." In dialogue we must have the shared intention of inquiry and a commitment to develop it deeper. This is why dialogue is not intended as a decision making modality.

As the opening quote suggests, if we are to be continuous learners co-creating today for the good of tomorrow, questions are the critical means for evolving our thinking and being. If we really believed this, we would be grateful for those colleagues who cared

enough to ask the hard questions. How open are we to these voices? Do we label and blame those voices for holding up our progress? Do we judge them as negative and resistant? How many of us are currently practicing to be masters of inquiry?

It is imperative for us to acknowledge our need for questions and value them even more than the answers we seek. For it is in the questions that we will spur each other's thinking to new heights--one question leading to another and another. This may be overwhelming if we think we have a responsibility to then find answers to all of them? As we learn the art of inquiry we realize that the generation of questions around a specific issue can open our thinking. If we tried to stop and answer each one, we may never get to the deeper issues. It is actually in the act of considering diverse questions that we have learning. Answers can be limiting unless we invite all possibilities and resist the temptation to accept the "right" answer too soon. There may be multiple answers or even no answers. Can we accept those possibilities?

Some things exist as a mystery for a reason. Some answers do not emerge because we are not ready to find them. Rachel Naomi Remen (1996) in her book called *Kitchen Table Wisdom*, gives an example of this insight. A cancer patient is relaying a meaningful story he heard to Dr. Remen, who is his physician. The story involves God and an angel in training. The angel sees a starving, poor man on earth and asks God why he doesn't provide the man with a bag of gold. God answers that the man is not ready for the gold he will not recognize it. The angel questions further until God places a bag of gold right in the man's path. The man looks at the bag and continues walking, wondering what good that bag of stones would have done for him. Dr. Remen asked the patient if he had experienced any bags of gold in his life and he replied, "My cancer?" How many times do we fail to see the gold in our experiences? We wonder, in asking the meaningful questions, are we living more meaningful answers?

Those of us who have never really thought of using questions in this way have to exercise our abilities and experiment with bringing inquiry into our work cultures. It is important to note that the use of inquiry can be practiced and evolved in any interaction,

meeting, discussion, or dialogue. We have gained insights around introducing inquiry into many health care settings, especially in interdisciplinary councils where caregivers, managers, educators, and even patients come together to build shared meaning and explore thinking and being.

In what ways can the notion of inquiry be introduced into our work settings? Just as the introduction to this chapter has indicated, we need to raise awareness about questions to our colleagues. Though each of us can practice inquiry skills with our own thinking, it is important to introduce the notion of inquiry and explain our intentions as we proceed with our interactions with others. The reason for this is to avoid misinterpretation of why questions are suddenly being asked when they have not been before. Sometimes colleagues become defensive because they interpret questions as threatening or disruptive. We have to consider how questions are currently being used in our work settings and how people have reacted to them.

The intention of a question can be self serving when someone is asking it to expose a lack of knowledge in a colleague. It is important to check our own motivation for asking questions. Are we leading others to our thinking and trying to get them to "buy-in" to our way of thinking? Others can tell when they are being coerced or controlled by questions. If this has been prevalent in the culture, the introduction of inquiry for genuine learning and exploration may raise suspicion and will require a more cautious approach. Everyone must be willing to ask questions that have no answers, be surprised at responses, and be open to changing their thinking.

What is the role of inquiry during reflection and introspection? Questions are extremely effective in promoting personal introspection, growth, and transformation. Asking questions of oneself is the recommended place to begin to practice inquiry skills. Many have found it to be the key in shifting from a reactive to a proactive stance. The moment we feel the urge to react to someone's thinking, we can ask ourselves what this reaction is about before we respond. Our interactions become more respectful as we learn to question our own feelings rather than judge the views of others.

Inquiry can provoke a "Call to Action" and offers insights toward self growth. The poem on page 83 is an example of how introspective inquiry emerges.

In what ways can we use inquiry to clarify our purpose and actions? As cited earlier in the Principles of Partnership, relationships thrive when a group is synchronized in its collective mission. In health care settings, the mission is providing healing, health care services. How can groups grow together rooted in mission and purpose? The mission should drive our actions and daily work, but it may not happen if groups do not have the opportunity for meaningful conversations.

This is where dialogue can help. Because dialogue is not narrowed to fixing a problem or making a decision, it helps us uncover our individual and collective thinking and being. We have led thousands in the work of clarifying their personal mission as well as connecting in the purpose of their work with others. It has yielded profound realizations by many. Inquiry has been key in exploring this territory.

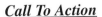

Call To Action

Listen to your voice of knowing
notice *how* it calls to you.

Hear the compelling triggers
shouting for attention, reflection, and action.

In the confusion...
Ask, Is this a normal part of growth?
Seek the deeper questions.

In the act of blaming...
Ask, How am I contributing to this?
Publicly disclose your insight.

In the act of apathy...
Ask, What brings purpose and meaning
to *my* life?
Tap courage and follow *your* path.

In the act of arrogance...
Ask, Who do I need help from?
Show your vulnerability.

In the act of defensiveness...
Ask, What is behind my reaction?
Be willing to change your thinking.

In the act of withdrawal...
Ask, What am I withdrawing from?
Reach out for connections.

Listen to your voice of knowing
Answer when it calls to you.

- Laurie Shiparski

First, we can consider mission and purpose on a personal level. People need time to step back from the busy pace of their work and reflect on what matters most to them in their lives. Thought provoking questions include: What gets you up in the morning? What brings joy to your life? What is your bliss? What do you fantasize about doing in your life? What need does your current work fill in your life? Why did you pursue this profession in the first place? What events led you to where you are now in life? This is not an exercise in leading people to conform to organizational values or mission. It is an exercise of remembering how we came to be where we are now, discovering meaning, and locating joy in life. It is only after we are clear on our personal mission that we can evaluate our synchronicity with the missions of our work place.

As a group seeks to develop shared meaning in their work, conversations take on a different feel from normal problem solving meetings. As we have brought groups together to do mission and vision work, it has been with the intention of creating a space for the collective thinking to emerge. This has been welcomed by people, and the most frequent comment after experiencing the process has been, "We have never come together to discuss this before, we were always handed a written mission and vision statement and told to live it or leave." It is not merely the outcomes of the written statements that hold the greatest value; it is the connections people make with each other during the process.

This work has been done by asking staff, managers, educators, and researchers in given areas to discuss and dialogue together on their collective mission and vision. We then have a time for all the departments or areas in the organization to present their mission and vision to others. Usually what emerges in such conversations are the many differences and similarities we share, as well as our hopes, dreams and disappointments.

The group work connects people. It positively shapes their future interactions and partnerships. During this process, reactions have surfaced. Some managers have reacted with concern as a group gets together and visions without predetermined boundaries. A reaction from staff has been apathy toward even trying such a process. These are symptoms of the hierarchy we are all trying to transcend.

When groups gather to present their mission and vision work, there is time for them to explore what they heard. The inquiry goes like this, What did you notice? What were the common themes? Did anything surprise you? Was anything missing? What did you learn about yourself? What did you realize about the group? It is in this conversation that the group grows deeper in shared thinking and being. Inquiry continues as they explore how they can live what they believe.

There is usually a gap between desired and current reality, a gap that frustrates and mystifies. So we ask ourselves, in what circumstances do we feel we can give the kind of care we envision? What holds us back from moving toward our vision and living our mission? In what ways are we currently seeing evidence of our core beliefs in daily practice? These, too, are discussions that are important in daily interactions and for exploration in dialogue.

We can learn to mirror what is occurring in the dialogue with questions. Many times in our meetings we barely have time to get through all of our issues, let alone notice much else about our meeting experience. Dialogue helps us to slow down and notice all that is occurring. An inquiry technique that has been very useful is that of mirroring back to the group what we see happening. This can be in the form of a question. Examples of occurrences to mirror back include:

- "I notice we are not asking questions of our own thinking; I wonder why that is?"

- "It feels as though our ideas are being quickly batted back and forth; does anyone else feel this?"

- "The energy in the room feels like it is winding down; what do you think?"

- "What is behind your thinking on that; is there a deeper issue?"

This is not inquiry reserved for the dialogue facilitator; all participants are completely present and cognizant of all that is occurring.

Polarity and disagreement can offer us a haven for inquiry. In some organizations we have found that polarity and disagreement are not welcomed perspectives.

In dialogue it is considered an opportunity for deeper inquiry and exploration. It is welcomed as a desired occurrence. For most of us, it takes readjusting of our own thinking to achieve a comfort level with disagreement. Through inquiry, it is possible to stop reactions and slow down long enough to listen to the views of others. We can ask, "What brought you to these realizations and beliefs?" It is in these rich words that we often hear our colleagues for the first time. In every situation where polarity exists, the learning and break through wisdom seems more profound. Questions that have been helpful in the midst of disagreement include:

- How did you come to believe that?

- That's an interesting perspective, I wonder...?

- In what other life experiences have you encountered this feeling, situation, circumstance? How did you respond then?

- I'm really trying to take in what you are saying and you have stimulated me to think about...

- Your question has stimulated another question for me...

Instead of defending or withdrawing during disagreement, we are called to open our thinking and seek clarification from others on their thinking. In these situations, questions are most useful. *In the face of disagreement we are signaled to uncover our common ground.* In these moments of impasse, it has been helpful to pause and have each person briefly share his/her current perspective. After hearing each voice, clarity emerges as each voice offers a piece of the collective puzzle.

Too much agreement is also a signal for us to use inquiry. Many of us jokingly say, "If everyone would just agree with us, things would be so much easier." Easier, yes, but also boring, confined, and lacking in possibilities. Beware of a dialogue or interaction where there is too much agreement. I'm noticing we all agree on this, why do you think that is? In the hierarchical cultures it can indicate fear to disagree.

There may also be assumed shared meaning in common words that need to be validated within the group. Listen for the words that we assume shared meaning and ask what does this really mean to each of us? Some common words we have encountered include trust, support, quality, partnership, and values. In one dialogue session we were discussing humanism. It was being used by many, but some were really unsure what it meant and felt compelled to ask, "What does it really mean to be human in the work place? Is it possible not to be human?" We each knew what it meant personally, but once others disclosed their perspectives, we uncovered divergent assumptions.

Wisdom From The Field

As a final note on the use of inquiry, we offer a story about a group of about 15 people who came together in their first dialogue session and uncovered a realization that evoked a long deep silence as they recognized the implications of a question. The session began with discussion about the question, "What support do we need from our system to live our core values?" In the beginning there was blaming and unhappiness about the current system.

Gradually, as they experimented with inquiry, things went deeper. Even though they did not get to the point of true dialogue, someone asked a thought provoking question that stopped everyone in their tracks. The following poem, "Who Is The System," offers the essence of this session. In the end, dialogue revitalized this group's sense of empowerment and hope.

Who Is The System?

There are so many reasons why
we can't reach our goals set high.

The system is always a good thing to blame
it has worked us and left us tired and lame.

So here we are feeling vengeful and helpless,
sharing pity and blame in the stifling stress.

We gather together to find our way out
when suddenly a question raises some doubt.

This system that has such a paralyzing hold
who is it and how is it strong and so bold?

A realization emerges with silence and a hush;
it is clear that the system really is us.

The system is us.

- Laurie Shiparski

PRINCIPLE OF DIALOGUE: SILENCE
What is the nature of silence and what usefulness does it offer?

Silence Noticed

An odd thing is silence, invisible if we let it.
A wonder to admire, a mystery to enjoy.
Yearned for and yet resented.
When noticed, it shows many personalities...
In its peacefulness,
feel the softness of a child asleep in your arms.
In its stillness,
feel the emptiness of a dead corpse.
In its exuberance,
feel the uncovering of a surprising truth.
In its heaviness,
feel the thick fear that mutes the voices of truth.
In its numbness,
feel the apathy of souls that have given up
their life's energy.
In its solitude,
experience an inviting place of no time or space.
Silence...
- Laurie Shiparski

*H*ave you ever been in a meeting or situation when silence occurred and you wondered why it felt so uncomfortable? Did you have the urge to break the silence with humor, or by changing the subject? Did you notice others' discomfort? Have you ever asked yourself in those situations, I wonder what this silence really means? At one time or another we have all accepted silence in our lives without taking the time to notice all it has to tell us. In learning more about dialogue we have gained a great appreciation for the many personalities of silence. It is a very useful occurrence if we seek its purpose and befriend it.

As the opening poem bespeaks, there are different kinds of silence--these are only a few. We will explore these aspects of silence in hopes of inviting others to use it in deepening dialogue experiences in the work place.

In many ways, silence is a sacred occurrence. Silence is the unnoticed quality of our life. We have discovered it to be essential to enriching our spiritual lives. In Native American and Eastern cultures, silence is a necessity of life. They purposefully expose themselves to days or years of silence. Many of us have realized a need for it and seek it in nature walks in the woods or time on a remote beach. During the past few years meditation, prayer, mindfulness, and

contemplation have become popular topics. All include the use of silence. How many of us are noticing its presence, or lack of presence, in our daily lives?

Silence is many things including: wordlessness, utter stillness, serenity, secrecy, quiet, muteness, and the act of not speaking. In dialogue we learn to first notice the silence and then seek its meaning in the moment. Those gathered in its presence usually know exactly what personality is presenting. We need only ask ourselves, "What does this silence represent?"

In dialogue we accept and welcome silence, but for many of us it takes perseverance to become comfortable in the midst of it. We are not used to just being in it and enjoying it. For some, silence is actually embarrassing when it occurs in a group. It is embarrassing because we are not sure what to do in it. We might do the wrong thing and embarrass ourselves even more. We must invite others to look at silence in a different way. We can produce it and become acquainted with it in dialogue and private moments.

In time, silence will become more familiar and we may be able to leave behind the urge to "break" it. Charlotte Roberts, in *The Fifth Discipline FieldBook* by Senge et al. (1994), recommends that we actually call for a period of silence during times of heated discussion or confusion. This is a useful tool in many circumstances.

We must explore the times when silence naturally emerges. We will attempt to describe how some silences feel as they occur in dialogue. There has already been a chapter offered on listening that goes hand in hand with silence. It is in the deep listening that the different types of silence can be identified.

The still, empty space feeling of silence occurs around dialogue sometimes when the group is hesitant to begin or is unsure of what to say. This is very common when participants have just learned about dialogue principles and are hesitant to try them because they might do something wrong. It is an opportunity to reassure people that there is no right or wrong way to do dialogue because it is meant to be learning in action. Every experience is considered learning and there are no mistakes.

In its heaviness, silence can represent a thick fear that mutes the voices of truth. This can occur in pre-dialogue situations where participants have such a great fear of speaking that there is dead silence. If this feeling of silence continues very long, we will often ask what the silence represents. We can invite that one voice of courage to break the silence and bring the truth of the situation to light. This has been a frequent occurrence in cultures of strong hierarchy and control. Very often the perceived fear is greater than the actual threat. We are reminded of a quote from American writer Naomi Wolf, "...only one thing is more frightening than speaking your truth. And that is not speaking." Dialogue is a way to move past the fear in silence.

In its numbness, silence can harbor the apathy of souls that have given up their life's energy. The apathy feels lighter than the fear. When this silence is present, the group can relocate their pulse of hope through dialogue. In working with apathetic groups, they have been revived by listening to each other during dialogue. They realize they are not alone but are in this together and they can support each other. At the conclusion of dialogue, when each person shares their key learning, it often reflects the group's transformation from apathy to hope. We also cannot underestimate the power of naming the nature of the apathy so that a group can find ways to move through it.

In its exuberance, silence is the uncovering of a surprising truth. In dialogue, this is a wonderful moment of epiphany and awe. It is when something is uncovered, and it provokes a stillness as participants bask in the realization of the learning. Sometimes in this silence we have the urge to move into a planning mode because this insight has the potential to change everything. It is best to savor this moment. More experienced groups, engaged in dialogue and feeling the collective wisdom, will sit in silence as what has been said churns in the center.

Talking is not the only way to engage in dialogue. Silence can be a time of deepening our own thinking and feeling the collective connection within the group. During one dialogue there was a great sense of peace surrounding us. Silence was there for us to feel the serenity and nourish our Spirit.

Because dialogue is reflective, it teaches us to seek the quiet space within ourselves. Once we make time for silence in our lives, we are to wait and listen in this space. We listen for that within us that needs to be given voice. It is in this solitude and peacefulness that we find the food that grows us beyond belief. Sometimes in this silence we hear internal voices that are unsettling to us. As we seek growth, the voice within may guide us in directions that we had not planned. Joseph Campbell (1988) reminds us, "We must be willing to get rid of the life we've planned so as to have the life that is waiting for us."

We can use silence to listen and seek clarity in the midst of our chaos. We realize that to grow we must experience both clarity and chaos. They occur as expected, never ending cycles. We are assured that we are growing as we endure these cycles of clarity and chaos. If we listen, there is direction. In the silence lies great wisdom calling our attention, but competing with the noise in our lives. It takes patience to clear the clutter in our minds to make way for this wisdom to emerge. It is important to consider how many Native

American people have practiced dialogue for hundreds of years. They are comfortable in silence and only speak when their spirit moves them to speak.

We are also reminded of this silence as we care for patients in health care settings. In being completely present with a patient, we have used silence even more powerfully than words. Our silent presence conveys that we are there with them totally and completely--no words are needed. Many have sat with grieving families in silence, not because we did not know what to say, but because we were immersed in the moment with them. This presence is the greatest gift we can give each other as human beings. In relationship building with others, it offers a connection deeper than words.

There is a standing invitation for us to notice, evoke, and use silence in our work places and lives. We can use it to relieve the pressure of fear, to celebrate the uncovering of a truth, and to rekindle the flame of hope and empowerment. It is there for us to access the space of wisdom that resides in each one of us. Silence cannot continue to be considered a waste of time or not worthy

of our attention. Those who notice silence and seek to know it more intimately will experience a richness and clarity about the essence of being human.

Mother Theresa (1996) has offered us perspective on silence in this prayer which she asked to be sent worldwide.

"The fruit of silence is
PRAYER.
The fruit of prayer is
FAITH.
The fruit of faith is
LOVE.
The fruit of love is
SERVICE.
The fruit of service is
PEACE."

LIVING DIALOGUE:
Can dialogue offer hopeful outcomes for the work place?

Learning To Live In The Gap

The gap is where
we now live and breathe,
a place between
current and desired reality.

We've tried to live
in this gap so wide
striving to predict, measure,
and sometimes hide.

When will we get there,
arrive at the end?
How will we prove it,
with our dreams to defend?

It's not about achieving
an end in sight
for as soon as we reach it
we see a new field of flight.

It is about being, living on
this eternal continuum,
learning and growing
now and to come.

- Laurie Shiparski

 W hy should we take the time to learn and grow in this way? Dialogue is not another theme of the month. How many of us have become disillusioned with themes, projects, and programs that seem to fragment our work and confuse us? We search for a quick fix to our problems. There are no fast answers. Many of us get entangled in the busyness of our environment. We feel pressure to do more in less time. "We don't have time to build relationships, there's too much to do." This is a frequently heard comment. The ongoing support for us to connect is missing. There is often no time nor place for us to practice genuine ways to be together and methods to move deeper in our relationships and connections. We are avoiding the very foundational work that can change these cycles of frustration.

Dialogue can help. It is very different from past approaches that taught us how to keep everyone on track through group facilitation skills. Many of us learned them well and measured our success by how well we adhered to the agenda and how many decisions we could make in one meeting. This has led to the development of common cultures across the continent that unintentionally shut down those who bring opposing views, and opportunities for meaningful listening and discussion. This was a useful phase to have lived through, because it offered learning and a context within which to differentiate dialogue. Now it is time to move forward and enhance our partnerships at higher levels. Dialogue thrives on diverse views, and it can refocus people on "I." A reminder to change themselves to make a difference.

How can using dialogue strengthen the threads of connection within a group? In what ways can dialogue expand the capacity of a group to thrive during change? These questions may be difficult to measure through our standard measurement methods. No matter what the measurements show, it is best to listen as a group articulates if they feel stronger and more connected. Their perceptions are their reality. In groups where cohesion is high they feel like they can accomplish anything. They have bonded together in strength to support each other and accomplish their work. We have listed below some specific changes or shifts experienced by groups who have experimented with dialogue. These shifts have expanded individual and group capacity.

The Paradoxical Shifts

Surfaced In Dialogue		Outcomes For Participants
Expose fear.	⇒	Decreases individual and collective fear. Uncovers hope to transcend fear.
Expose differences. ("We are so different.")	⇒	Uncovers differences and common ground, increased cohesion.
Expose vulnerability.	⇒	Builds a force field of invulnerability for individual and group. Increases group cohesion.
Expose diverse perspectives.	⇒	Uncovers new options.
Comfort in confusion. (Less worried about keeping conversation on track.)	⇒	Unrelated things come together and lead to surprising insights. Connects diversity and brings new insights.
Individuals feel distant & withdraw. (Apathy and blame are symptoms.)	⇒	Individuals extend an invitation to each other for participation and connection. Group capacity and hope is tapped.
Arrogance - "We know."	⇒	Element of surprise reaffirms there is an abundance not known. Expands potential capacity for change.

We are learning to shift from destructive cycles to positive cycles of growth. It takes time to perpetuate positive or negative cycles. People in organizations work side by side and perpetuate destructive cycles of being together. An example of this kind of cycle is when an incident occurs that feels unjust to a group and they bond around that incident.

As Carolyn Myss (1994) notes in her presentation, "Why People Don't Heal," we can bond in our wounds and never pass through them. We must try to live a full life in spite of what has happened to us. Our wounds cannot be an excuse to become paralyzed and hopeless. She points out that this risk can present in support groups where people may keep each other in the pain and not move through it.

Sometimes, if an individual does take the bold step forward to transcend his/her pain, he/she may be ostracized from the group. This phenomenon happens in organizations and in many of our personal lives right now. We are often not aware of it, or unwilling to name it.

In our experience with organizations,

people are developing their own informal support groups of pain that are perpetuating destructive cycles. Because we cannot move through the pain, we stay in it and spend our time fixing the symptoms. This is no different from when we experience a hardship in our personal lives.

In the midst of trying times we have to reach deep down inside ourselves to summon the courage, perseverance, and compassion to move forward. It is then important to reach out to others. Will we come through these times feeling stronger than ever with a greater belief in our abilities of endurance or will we let these times cripple our spirit and continue life feeling miserable and unfulfilled? It is our choice.

The diagrams on page 107 illustrate how these cycles differ and how dialogue has provided a basis for us to derail the destructive cycles. Dialogue offers new ways of thinking and being that we can learn and use to create constructive cycles.

We have noticed that after embracing these principles of dialogue we even shift out of perceiving incidences as negative. Over time we realize that all experiences are valuable and occur to teach us something.

Destructive Cycle

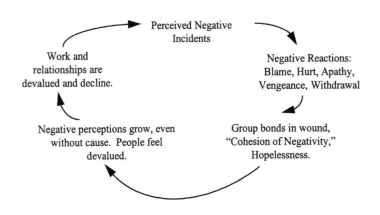

Perceived Negative
Incidents

Work and
relationships are
devalued and decline.

Negative Reactions:
Blame, Hurt, Apathy,
Vengeance, Withdrawal

Negative perceptions grow, even
without cause. People feel
devalued.

Group bonds in wound,
"Cohesion of Negativity,"
Hopelessness.

Constructive Creative Cycle
(Dialogue Foundation In Place)

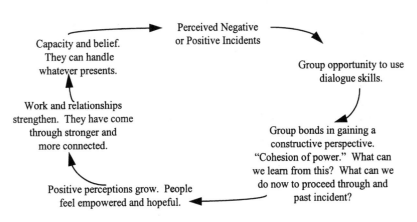

Perceived Negative
or Positive Incidents

Capacity and belief.
They can handle
whatever presents.

Group opportunity to use
dialogue skills.

Work and relationships
strengthen. They have come
through stronger and
more connected.

Group bonds in gaining a
constructive perspective.
"Cohesion of power." What can
we learn from this? What can we
do now to proceed through and
past incident?

Positive perceptions grow. People
feel empowered and hopeful.

Our negative reactions may still happen, but we quickly convert to checking our assumptions using inquiry, listening, and generating collective learning. We can keep our perceptions in check and prevent them from spiraling out of control. Rumors no longer stoke the flames of misunderstanding. In this context, relationships are not considered the fluff, but the vital element to perpetuating creative cycles. The following Wisdom From The Field excerpt portrays the conversion from a destructive to a creative cycle through the use of the principles of dialogue.

Wisdom From The Field

A group of staff from a patient care unit of a hospital had developed a Unit-Based Council where they could practice using dialogue skills, learn to be better partners with each other, and make decisions about their practice and work environment. Over a two year period they had learned about these ways of thinking and being from the Clinical Practice Model framework (Wesorick, 1996). They had experienced workshops on partnership and dialogue, and read materials on changing their culture and their system to support this new thinking. They were trying new ways of communicating and being together in daily interactions as well as in the Unit Council, which was the ongoing infrastructure for exploring leadership and partnership together on a regular basis.

The manager was a member of this Council and represented an equal voice in decision making. She brought the expertise of managing the operation's aspect of the unit while the staff represented their expertise in patient care. Together they were on the road to shifting their relationships from hierarchy and bureaucracy to partnering. They were questioning and changing previous boundaries of decision making. There had been successes, and the perceptions on the unit were changing. This work on relationships was shifting negative, apathetic feelings to positive, productive feelings. Together they worked on seemingly unsolvable issues that had been lingering for years and, through the use of dialogue, uncovered deeper insights that offered ways to finally resolve them.

This was difficult work, but they knew it was going to be worth it. It had to be energy well spent because before learning these

ways, most of their energy was used up in the fight. They had been desperate because the morale on the unit was very low. They found themselves caught up in a destructive cycle where the manager thought the staff were not taking accountability, and the staff thought the manager was controlling and dictatorial. The more the manager mistrusted the staff, the more the staff mistrusted her. Even though the unit budget statistics looked fine and patient care was functionally acceptable, the patients were beginning to complain as they would overhear staff concerns. As each person on the council began to work on his/her own thinking and behavior, their collective morale got better. As each person changed his/her perceptions, the collective perceptions shifted to the positive, constructive cycle. Things were not perfect, but they seemed to be changing for the better.

In the midst of their successful work, an event happened that jeopardized all of the progress made to this point. A practice decision implemented by the Unit Council was rejected by the physicians. The hospital administration tried to be an intermediary, pleasing both sides. Unfortunately, the long standing power of the physicians won over and the system implemented was to be immediately stopped.

At first the Council members felt angry, betrayed, powerless, vengeful, and hopeless. This dark cloud had arrived over their heads and was about to obliterate their new found collective power. The following comments were changing the dark cloud into the beginnings of a funnel cloud. "Why do we bother anyway? We are just kidding ourselves; we can't make a difference here in this place. All that work we did, down the tubes. I give up. We really are alone; we can't muster up enough power together to impact anything. Who is to blame for this? We'll show the physicians; wait until they need us." The tornado of hopelessness was forming. At this point, it could still be stopped.

The Unit Council members convened and began to ask questions of each other. "How did this happen? What is the real story versus the rumor mill story? What learning can we gain from this experience? What can we do now as a collective?" They were tapping their new found capacity. In the end, this experience ended up bonding them together.

They came through the dark cloud even stronger than before. They realized they had not been the best partners with the physicians. They were reminded that years of hierarchy would not be obliterated overnight. They collectively accessed their courage and perseverance to give voice to that which needed to be addressed.

The Council stopped a tornado from forming because even the other units that were not involved had heard about the incident and were now questioning what else the physicians could take away. This small group of people initiated an organization intervention that turned a potentially devastating incident into one of growth and progress. They met with the other Councils and clarified the true story to stop rumor generation. They met with the physicians to discuss the process, decision, and possible options for resolution. They were able to modify their plan and desired outcome and still implement the changes.

Some would criticize this Council, saying they should have planned better in the first place. They would blame the group and not see the incident as a successful, necessary event. If this incident had never happened, the Council would not have been able to identify their new capacity and unity.

In life, everything happens for a reason. Instead of questioning why something happens, we need to ask, "What are we to learn?" It is like the seed of a tree that struggles to push through the soil, not knowing why it needs to struggle, but understanding that strife is part of growing.

In all of nature, this is the pattern of growth. Even in the human being, birth can be a trying experience, hence the term "labor." The worries do not end after birth. Raising children is also challenging, but we do not stop having them because it is too difficult. Why do we reject this pattern in the growth of our own work places? In nature, a struggle often translates as progress; in our personal growth and organizational growth, struggles often translate into setbacks. This evokes a critical question, "In what ways do our struggles strengthen and prepare us for experiences to come?"

When and how can we change ourselves and our work places? There is a call for intimacy in the work place, a humaniza-

tion of what has for many become a transactional numb part of life or a drain on their BodyMindSpirit. For those who are energetically and passionately changing things for the better, they need sustenance. In producing creative cycles through dialogue, we change our cultures and our ways of being together. There has been learning generated around the nature of change and the development of methods to support us in transforming our work cultures. The next two chapters will explore this learning as well as ways to introduce and perpetuate the use of dialogue.

LIVING DIALOGUE:
In what ways can dialogue
motivate us to change?

A hand moves, and the fire's whirling
takes different shapes.
...All things change when we do.
The first word, Ah, blossomed into all others.
Each of them is true.
- Zen Master Kukei

*H*ow often in your work place have you witnessed or participated in a change process? Have we not all lived change, daily? Have you said or heard statements like these? We need to find a way to get "buy-in." They have to learn to accept change, get over it, and move on. We have to plan this well so no disruption is felt--control all the variables. We were not ready for this; it is over our heads. Even though I like change, it is still hard. Who is doing this to us anyway? Why is this happening to me?

Each of these statements reflects deeper issues and beliefs about change. There are individual beliefs that keep work groups

swirling at the surface of deeper issues in the midst of their meetings and interactions. These are beliefs that are brought to work as part of our being whether we want to recognize them or not. Assumptions buried deep within us continue to surface and manifest in our behaviors, so why not surface them through dialogue and use them constructively?

We cannot continue to live in change and depend on our old ways of thinking and doing to get us through. It is not that we do not seek innovative ways. In most organizations, people long for ways to thrive in change. How can we notice and name these beliefs in order to view change in a different light?

Dialogue offers ways to uncover our collective learning about change. Acknowledging this is key to our progress. We have the wisdom within our collective experiences. Why then are we always searching outside of ourselves for the answers? Consider the following story that illustrates wisdom from the field generated during a dialogue session as a group uncovered its collective learning.

Wisdom From The Field

A group of approximately 50 people gathered for a two hour dialogue to explore the question, *What is the nature of change?* This group, whose positions centered on being change agents, represented over 30 health care settings across the United States and Canada. They had one thing in common, a mission to collectively create empowered, healing health care environments.

Many of them had not experienced dialogue before and were using this time to practice the principles outlined in this book. They were also anticipating the learning of new insights regarding the issues of change. It is important to note that each participant regarded the others as having an equal voice in what was about to unfold.

It was an energetic discussion which transitioned into dialogue near the end. At first, there were many issues and perspectives surfacing and it was difficult to see how they connected. The pace of talking was quick, without many breaks of silence in between the speaking. Insights offered seemed to bounce around the room like a ping pong ball, which is very typical in early

phases of learning dialogue.

After approximately an hour, the pace slowed and some of the issues brought were connecting to produce collective wisdom. Inquiry and listening deepened as the superficial comments converted into rich words of the heart. The energy in the room was high as many shared their personal insights and experiences of pain and joy during change. The individual perspectives surfaced to weave a collective pattern that changed many of us forever.

How did a dialogue of this nature change our behavior? A realization emerged: *Change is the state of being in life, and without change there would be no life.* This was powerful for many; it was a freeing thought for some, and at the same time a terrifying thought for others. Change was not a burden to bear; it was life itself. How different our approaches to planning change would be if we operated from this belief. We realized that change was out of our control. The more we tried to control it, the harder it became to live in it. Of course we realized we still needed to plan change in our lives and organizations, but now we were challenged to consider the possibility that everything happened for a reason.

Have "unsuccessful" changes occurred to teach us something? What is it that we learn in the struggles? What would life be without them? And why were we trying to save others from feeling the pain of change? In fact, we realized during the painful times we grew the most. This realization alone impacts how we might plan organizational change in the future. Should we continue to avoid disruption, or gain a level of comfort with it? Even expect it and welcome it as a successful outcome.

We also surfaced the realization that we had control over one thing in change and that was ourselves. If we wanted to change others, we needed to <u>begin by changing ourselves first</u>. As this dialogue ended, we were exhilarated by the uncovering of new directions and at the same time tired from the intense listening, assumption checking, and inquiring.

We live in cultures with more emphasis on doing together than being together. It is not often we experience the level of conversation at work that occurs in dialogue, because we are all too busy doing together instead of being together. Can we afford not to have such experiences? How would our interactions be different if we were uncovering foundational learning together that would change how we do everything? This is not to imply that "doing" is undesirable; we need a balance of being together and doing together. The doing should flow from our being together.

If we do not take the time to dialogue on the front end, we will double our time in the doing on the back end. If our doing is not synchronized, excess energy is spent seeking why something happened, who is to blame, and fixing what went wrong. The verse on page 121 offers reflection on this issue.

In what way would the work place feel different? Think about when a family is planning a vacation to a remote destination. They might wonder, "What will we do when we get there? What will keep us busy?" On such a vacation a family may experience a slowing down from their normal fast paced lives. Being together without activities every moment would feel uncomfortable at first; it may seem like they are not doing enough.

Front End Or Back End

Lets get it done
take care of this issue,
This problem must be fixed.
Don't hesitate, get on it now.
We need to act real quick!

Let's celebrate the work you've done.
The quick fix has occurred.
A slap on the back,
a new position or
feedback is your reward.

Tomorrow is here
and things are done,
But something's not quite right!
How much work
do you think it will take
to undo what we've just done?

- Bonnie Wesorick

By the second day, the discomfort dissipates and a relaxed feeling surfaces. There is genuine joy experienced in just being with one another and getting reacquainted. There is no time pressure, no stress, nor lack of patience. Discussion emerges and each member has a chance to talk about views without being in the midst of an issue related to his/her thinking.

This is not to say that being together in this way always feels wonderful, steady, and stable. In the slowing down, each family member is invited to put out thinking and actually have others listen uninterrupted. Heated discussions may occur, but there is no pressure to resolve an issue or make a decision.

This scenario reminds us that at the heart of successful change is the work of relationships. The principles of partnership reviewed earlier in this book offer a context to question our current relationships. Dialogue offers a means for people to gain fresh insights into individual and group change. These are strategies to help people deepen their understanding and strengthen their capacity to effectively live change.

How has dialogue helped individuals and groups change? Answering this question is like asking new parents how having a child has changed their lives. Dialogue changes the very fabric of our being and doing. Through dialogue, personal change occurs because a person uncovers a learning from within themselves. This learning or realization is usually foundational to the individual's perspective on life. It is change "from the inside out." It becomes a part of who we are as a human being.

In this respect, teaching in the context of dialogue is uniquely different from formal education. In dialogue, we create a space where people experience their own learning. In this learning they are motivated to change from within, not because someone told them to do so, but because they have had their own epiphany. *This provokes two questions, "How can we bring learning experiences that offer both new thinking (through the offering of information) combined with dialogue (time for people to internalize the thinking)?" "In what ways can we do this to collectively grow new information beyond its current boundaries?"*

In the opening quote we are reminded that "All things change when we do." Knowing this may not be enough which provokes the question, "How do we get people to change so that all other things will change?" The answer lies in the understanding that we do not get other human beings to change. All of the best planning, communicating, and even coercing will not change a person who does not *choose* to change. To change oneself is a personal choice. Fox (1941) states, "The door of the soul opens inward and the answer to motivating environments lies within the person."

Dialogue can offer the opportunity for a person to hear the perspectives of others and examine his/her own thinking. Like it or not, we have to acknowledge that the power of acting on this learning sits with each individual. Dialogue has stimulated many to start new internal dialogues that continuously roll. It starts with self questioning to uncover what is behind one's thinking and desired reaction. The verse on page 125 by Judy Brown reveals the power we have in making choices.

It is important to notice and name our assumptions. Frequently in our interactions we fall into the trap of jumping to conclusions about the words and behaviors of others. We either agree or disagree with what is being said or done. Often we think we know exactly where a person is coming from with their thinking. Based on knowing where a person is coming from, we make judgments and take action. At times we do understand the other person, and sometimes we are misunderstanding them. This has often been the case as situations escalate out of control between people. How can we stop this cycle of misconception?

Choosing

Choosing.

The word stares back at me,
the center "O's" like gentle eyes,
just looking up at me
from this blank page.

Choosing.

Inquiring eyes.
"What are you choosing
in your life?" they seem to ask.
I look away.
Still those two eyes
hold steady, gaze inquiring,
wondering, "What do you choose?"

"I haven't got a lot of choice,"
I say. "The choices have already
come and gone and now my life
is in the doing not the choosing."

"Of course," the eyes say gently,
with compassion. "So you say.
But if you could choose again
with all the wisdom
that your life has brought,
what would your choice be now?"

I answer with quick certainty:
"That water's long gone underneath
the bridge, or is it o'er the dam.
(I never can remember which.)
The train has left the station,
and the horse has fled the barn.
The choosing is all done."

"Of course, the eyes of choosing
say to me, and gently, "But in
the river of your life right now,
within that flow, how do you choose?"

- Judy Brown

In learning and practicing the checking of assumptions, we are called to notice and name our internal theories, ideas, and beliefs. It is our thinking that drives all behaviors. Through dialogue we stop jumping to conclusions and learn to wait. We open ourselves to hear diverse perspectives instead of judging them right or wrong and then reacting. We ask ourselves, "What is evoking this reaction or nonreaction in me? What is behind my thinking? What experiences have led me to believe what I know?" We suspend our judgment, listen, and use inquiry to clarify what we think we are hearing, seeing, or feeling. This Wisdom From The Field is a personal story that illustrates the power of checking assumptions in the ongoing work of relationships.

Wisdom From The Field

I (Laurie Shiparski) had been in my Director role on a patient unit for about two months. I was just getting to know the work team that I had newly joined, and they were getting to know me. I had transferred from another unit in the hospital, and even before coming to the new team, they had developed assumptions about me. The word from my previous unit was that I lived partnership with others, had a high level of integrity, and demonstrated a genuine respect for others.

After the first months, the team began to question these initial assumptions. I was attending committees and council meetings that were previously for staff only. Destructive, mistrusting cycles developed as I tried to understand why the staff acted angrily and protective in their work. In one meeting a person even stated I was not welcome at the staff meeting. This was a moment of opportunity. I used inquiry to understand their thinking and check my thinking with the group.

I began by asking why they did not want me at the meetings. They told me that their previous manager did not attend the meetings because she trusted them to work through the issues, and they liked it that way. In their response I realized that my actions had been misinterpreted.

I then shared my thinking with the group. Clarifying my intentions as a partner in my role, I explained that I attended the meetings assuming that others would know

I was there to be a support and resource as operational issues arose. I wanted to work with the team. My intentions were good, but sadly misunderstood. The more I had tried to show support, the more the staff saw control and mistrust in my actions.

We were all surprised at how wrong our assumptions had been. Once this discussion occurred, our relationships in the team changed dramatically. We clarified with each other what partnership looked like in our work together and a cycle of trust and respect began.

Within the months to come, the staff recognized the importance of having my input at the meetings. In our decisions and work we came to value having the expertise of care providers, manager, educator, researcher, and even patients. These voices offered more options and richer learning. Eventually, if these diverse perspectives were absent from a meeting, it was canceled and important decisions tabled until we could get the whole group together.

Clarifying the assumptions in this situation proved to be pivotal in the ongoing success of this work team. It is helpful if a group has a collective way of signaling to each other that assumptions need to be checked. As suggested in *The Fifth Discipline Fieldbook*, Senge et al. (1994), the "Ladder of Inference" is one such tool. When we jump to conclusions, it is like going up a ladder. Beginning with observations or words we move up the rungs as we process it against our own experiences and thinking. Once up the ladder we can also walk ourselves right back down. When a group learns about the "Ladder of Inference," they refer to it in their interactions. For example, "After hearing what you said, I went right up my ladder. I'd like to clarify my thinking with you."

It is important to consider this in conjunction with the powerful skills of advocacy and inquiry which are addressed in this book. A worksheet used by thousands during presentations to examine their thinking and surface assumptions is provided on page 55.

What is the role of vulnerability in our relationships and in dialogue? Recognizing and using vulnerability requires crucial consideration to strengthening individuals and groups. In dialogue sessions, a phenomenon

occurs that has happened again and again. If one person shows vulnerability and speaks from the heart, it acts as an invitation to all the others and many will follow the lead. If vulnerability is not shared by at least one person, dialogue will be blocked.

Vulnerability is a human characteristic that holds both power and weakness at the same time. It has surfaced as a way to enhance individual capacity and form meaningful relationships. It is the glue that bonds us in being together in more genuine ways. It has a noticeable presence in dialogue sessions.

A question emerges: "If vulnerability is so effective, why are so many of us reluctant to show our vulnerabilities?" We can begin to understand our reaction by exploring the feelings this word evokes in us. When recognizing a vulnerability, have you ever felt exposed, open to attack, disadvantaged or burdened? Has fear accompanied these feelings? For most of us the *perceived consequences* of sharing our vulnerabilities with others seems to outweigh the benefits.

What perspective on vulnerability might hold a different value? In observing those who use vulnerability as a strength, an interesting phenomenon seems to occur. *In the act of exposing a personal truth from the soul, the vulnerability is converted to invulnerability.* To be invulnerable is to feel secure, indestructible, and protected. This occurs because what some call a weakness is present in a person whether he/she discloses it or not. If it is not disclosed, then the risk rests in the chance that it will surprisingly be uncovered by others through behaviors and interactions. If uncovered this way, a person may become defensive, angry, or withdraw with others.

What do we think about those who have disclosed a truth about themselves? *The ability to show your vulnerability is a hallmark of personal maturity and indicates a person has a clear sense of emotional safety.* His/her safety comes from within and is not dependent on what others think about him/her. This makes the person invulnerable with others.

We have witnessed many moments of people sharing a personal truth and every time it has yielded great wisdom. It always evokes attention and gratitude from others. As one person described, "Just before I am about to disclose such a truth, I feel a compelling anxiousness within. I have come to recognize this feeling and trust it. It is not fear of disclosing; it is not weakness, nor is it risk. It is a feeling of power and truth. It is often what others may know but are not revealing." Those who find vulnerability threatening are producing their own fear about it. *Ironically, the only way to transcend the fear is to make known our vulnerability.*

How can one find the courage to begin this process? We begin by acknowledging our own vulnerabilities and making a conscious decision to disclose them. In disclosure we are relieved of the intense use of energy and burden of hiding them. We can openly deal with the response of others on our own terms. To grow in relationships we must disclose them or others will not feel connected to us and in turn disclose their vulnerabilities. Thus, we go on being together in disconnected, erroneous ways. Consider the following personal story in this Wisdom From The Field.

Wisdom From The Field

As a manager, I (Laurie Shiparski) found myself becoming defensive whenever someone disagreed or criticized me. I was constantly judging myself better or worse than others--mostly better. I thought people might be picking up on these behaviors. My thoughts were confirmed one day when a caring colleague told me, "You don't have to discredit my situation just to make yourself look good." This was a wake up call for me to dig deeper and question why I needed to be right and the best all of the time.

This behavior was destroying my work and home relationships. After much soul searching I discovered that my defensiveness was a symptom of something deeper--a fear of rejection. If I wasn't chosen for a project or my idea was rejected, I became angry to cover up the hurt I was feeling inside. I eventually dug deeper to realize that my hurt began at birth when I was given up for adoption. For many years, this defensiveness was a part of my life and finally I was able to name it and work on eliminating it from my relationships.

I did not have to disclose all of these

details to show my vulnerability to others. There are ways to show vulnerability without disclosing all personal details. I did share with colleagues my discovery that my defensiveness was getting in the way of relationships and I had not intended that to happen. I admitted when I did not know something and asked for help. I stopped myself when the urge to be defensive arose and listened to the views and ideas of others.

Many of my colleagues now knew of my commitment to changing. They did not respond by taking advantage of me or capitalizing on my honesty. My actions did invite great levels of forgiveness, understanding, and admiration from others. The admiration came from others as they saw their own humanness in me. It took courage to admit my humanness. They respected me because I cared enough about myself and others to question my behavior and take accountability to change it.

The key to converting vulnerability to invulnerability is in the way in which we receive responses from others. If we are transforming ourselves to be less reactive to the judgment of others and more secure in who we are as individuals, we can build a transparent force field around our souls that deflects responses that would hurt us but allows others to see in. In being true to ourselves and honest with others, the force field gains strength.

The greatest fear of exposing a vulnerability is that another person will use it against us to maximize his/her own position. The support, love, and power of connection with people will strengthen each of so much that it will far outweigh this perceived fear. *For it is in the fear that we are really held captive by ourselves and others.*

In dialogue, groups can explore new ways to uncover and use key learning. Groups transform themselves through collective learning if they take the time to notice what learning they have uncovered. Dialogue strategies used in interactions and meetings yield learning and growth. How often are we quickly moving on to the next problem to fix without acknowledging what we have accomplished? If we do not take the opportunity to learn from our learning, we will not grow from our wisdom uncovered. This quote from Michael Jones (1995) calls us to change our current habits of doing and decision making, "I wonder how the rush to completion has short circuited our capacity to move in harmony with deeper cycles of creation."

To maximize our experiences we can learn from our learning. Many groups will record on a 3x5 card their key learning, insight or realization after a dialogue, and share them either verbally or in writing with each other. Everyone's voice is able to be read or heard and this learning always generates another level of learning. This technique can offer learning to others who were not even present at a meeting or dialogue. The following represents excerpts from such key learning. A group answered the question, "What have I learned about relationships during major change and chaos?"

- "Change promotes unity and division."
- "Connections with each other are everything."
- "Fear between us runs rampant."
- "Trusting each other is crucial."
- "I took relationships for granted before all this change."
- "I feel our sense of community dissipating."

- "Some relationships enrich--at the same time, some dissolve."

- "Conflict arises when there is competition versus a spirit of cooperation."

- "Reluctance to work on relationships during down sizing since the person may be gone tomorrow."

- "Mutual trust and respect must be there."

- "New relationships evolve."

- "It has become most important to listen to each other carefully."

- "Change brings the best and worst out in everyone, perception is everything."

- "It is a ton of work to maintain relationships during change."

- "Many withdraw and mistrust which decreases our will to work together."

- "Caring and nurturing each other is central."

- "Relationship building used to be a nice thing to have, now it seems like a life line."

It is curious to see the patterns of such wisdom generated from a group in the midst of an organizational transition and down sizing. This is happening in health care and other industries across the country. These voices are surfacing the feelings of many working in health care settings that we have encountered across the United States and Canada. The clear pattern here is that effective, fulfilling relationships are the key to successful, satisfying working environments. Why then, are organizations and the people in them, reluctant to spend time on relationship building?

For many of us, our quest to live meaningful lives in the midst of change continues. As individuals, if we utilize dialogue skills, work at introspection, and achieve personal change, we will begin to notice that our relationships grow and change for the better. Individual transition precedes group transition as human beings move toward deeper levels of understanding and connection. At times we may lose sight of this powerful concept, or doubt its truth, especially in the face of insurmountable change. In all circumstances we need only to believe the powerful words of Ghandi to find our pulse of hope again, "Each of us must be the change we want to see in the world."

LIVING DIALOGUE:
How can we experience dialogue in the work place?

"We seek out one another. Separate beings unite to create more complex beings. The separateness we thought we were creating melts into the unending dance of coadaptation and change as we become ever more aware of those from whom we cannot be separate."
- Wheatley and Kellner-Rogers

Can we miss something we have never had? There was a time when many could not have imagined using dialogue in the work place and now they cannot imagine the work place without dialogue. Our learning about dialogue has moved from seeing it as a new communication strategy to part of *being human*. For many it has moved from being viewed as relationship fluff to being as vital as breath to life. The word dialogue is somewhat over used right now and unless we clarify what we mean, others may think they have experienced it. Dialogue as outlined in this book, based on the principles of intention, advocacy, inquiry, listening, and silence, is what we

can now answer to those who ask, what is dialogue?

It has been difficult to introduce dialogue into work places because it is often not there. Because it feels different from our normal ways, we are uncomfortable at first. As Michael Jones (1995) points out in his book, *The Imaginative Life* "...doing what does not come naturally is a real test of courage...we must surrender to the process." That is surrender because we trust and believe that together in the right conditions, our collective wisdom will emerge. Dialogue is different because it is not a process we control; we come together and it emerges.

Even if some are not calling for dialogue, there is frustration with relationships and a longing for a different way of being together. But few have the courage and perseverance to truly commit to changing the way they have always done it. It is easier to endure apathy, anger, blame, and sabotage and seek quick fixes through implementing projects and programs. At least we can get our arms around those programs and feel like we are *doing* something constructive. The following poem offers insights on how some of our interactions in the work place feel.

Full and Empty

Our meetings are full
of schedules
timed talk and
quick decisions.

They are full
of words that swirl
at the surface
of deeper issues.

They are full
of giving information,
fixing problems,
and staying on track.

They are full
of ego building,
defending, blaming,
and judgment of others.

They are full
of quieting the voices
that bring questions and
unwanted truths.

Our meetings are full
and I am left empty.

Our meetings are full
and I am left empty.

Give me one clear
moment of silence
and the courage
to show my vulnerable self.

Let me be an invitation
for us to be together
in a meaningful,
genuine way.

- Laurie Shiparski

Does anyone experience dialogue negatively? There are some who say, "What is the big deal with this dialogue stuff anyway?" The experience does not speak to them as it does to others. This is not to be judged--the very essence of dialogue is one of invitation. Dialogue meets us where we are in our own personal journey. If we are not ready to open our hearts and minds to human conversations of this nature, dialogue will not be a deep experience for us. So this perspective is accepted, respected, and welcomed.

But, can we deny other human beings the opportunity to bring forth what needs to be given voice? Do we respect each other enough to listen to each voice? Just as this respect is given to those who do not find it helpful, it is imperative that they not block the experience for others. Dialogue is a very effective way for many people to learn and grow. It is also a way to honor others you are with by taking time to listen to their wisdom. We cannot rob others of this opportunity just because we have judged it invaluable. Some have been patient and gone to dialogues even though they were not sure they wanted to, and have surprisingly developed a comfort level for this kind of interaction. Many times in our lives we are unsure of things but are willing to experiment.

This chapter will offer insights from those who have successfully introduced and experimented with dialogue. There really is no right or wrong way to do dialogue, no prescribed format. However, there have been learning tools and approaches that have enabled many to shift into dialogue more easily. Some of us who have little value for the experience of dialogue may not have been persistent or patient enough with ourselves and others.

In what ways can dialogue be introduced and advanced? For those who have experienced it and are actively providing more opportunities in their organizations, dialogue has brought deep learning that far exceeds any formal education. Usually, after experiencing it, people become hungry for more. This hunger is like an awakening. We suddenly realize what has been missing. Even if we thought our work environment was progressive and good; after dialogue we realize how it can be even richer.

There have been growing communities

of dialogue all over the world. Some have had success by just starting with a small group in their organization which has expanded and branched out. Some have introduced the idea as an organization-wide commitment. Many communities have organized dialogue groups around such things as improving the health of their community. There are even international dialogue groups that come together. Some have begun in their smaller work areas. The following Wisdom From The Field enlightens us about how a patient care unit in a hospital began using dialogue principles to enrich their relationships and work.

Wisdom From The field

Only a few people on this patient care unit had learned and experienced dialogue, but they realized it would be a key strategy for the others in their work area to learn. They brought their learning and recommendation to the rest of those in their work area and a commitment was made for all to learn more. They put it into the strategic goals of the unit and developed a plan to introduce dialogue. The goal was to truly become a continuous learning group. A year's worth of education, exploration, and discussion culminated at their annual unit goal setting session, a time when the strategic initiatives were determined with staff, manager, and educator all in attendance. The difference this year was that they were not going to brainstorm and list goals and objectives as they usually did, but use dialogue to deepen their collective understanding before the planning.

The brainstorming format and subsequent multiple vote and rank ordering processes were perceived to have been very successful at previous retreats. There were concerns by the members that they would not accomplish the same objectives with the use of dialogue. However, they were willing to give it a try.

There was a leadership council on this patient care area called a Unit-Based Council. This Council was the infrastructure for staff, managers, and educators to develop their partnerships and involve everyone on the unit in decision making about improving their work environment and service to patients. The staff leader, staff educator, and

unit director spent time planning the process and selecting the location. Articles on dialogue were distributed to members in advance of the retreat to refresh their thinking and expand their knowledge. Much time was spent selecting a poem to read for the dialogue opening, and even more time was spent discussing what the opening question should be. It was decided to have the dialogue outside in a setting far removed from the hospital environment. A park with wetlands was chosen, and box lunches were ordered to create a picnic like atmosphere.

Council members met at the park and were escorted on a ten minute hike into the wetlands where dry ground and picnic space were located. Blankets were placed on the ground and members sat around in a circle eating their box lunches. A few key concepts of dialogue were reviewed, a check in was completed, the poem and question presented, meditation time honored, and the dialogue began.

The dialogue lasted for two hours and all members were actively engaged in the process. In keeping with time commitments, the dialogue was summarized and concluded within the two hour time frame. The themes that emerged and gave guidance to future Council initiatives during the dialogue included the following:

- Strengthen and enhance partnering relationships with patients, families, co-workers, and the multidisciplinary team.

- Create an environment where each team member is positively affirmed and encouraged to let his/her light shine.

- Continue the journey with dialogue.

Feedback from the Council members about the dialogue experience was overwhelmingly positive. The environment for the dialogue was peaceful. The earth brought out their sense of spirituality. During the dialogue, a jet flew overhead, and it reminded one member of the importance of keeping in touch with reality and remembering what they have available to them with the use of technology.

Other learnings included:
- The initial dialogue question did not make a difference. They learned that the important questions and wisdom emerge without the need to carefully craft an opening question. One person reflected on a ques-

tion she had heard recently when participating in a team member interview. The question centered on asking the interviewee to think of a shift on which they had worked after which they had gone home feeling especially rewarded and glad that they had chosen health care as their career. Others quickly picked up on this and much personal sharing occurred.

* Nature played a significant role in creating a learning atmosphere. Leaving the sheltered area by the parking lot and taking a ten minute walk to the destination gave each person time to debrief.

* It was important to summarize the key themes in the dialogue at the conclusion. This was surprisingly easy. There was a clear and common understanding as to what those themes were.

* The prior experiences with goal setting were also very productive, but the goals were rather superficial. Dialogue took them more to the heart of what they were about. It was easier to take the message back to unit team members.

* Dialogue saved them time. They accomplished their dialogue in two hours. The year prior, the brainstorming and decision making processes took four hours.

- The interdisciplinary team member expressed great appreciation for the use of dialogue and was awed by the wisdom she had gained from the experience. She presented the Council with a stone for use with future "check-ins" and remarked on how she had not experienced anything like this in her time at the hospital.

- Experiencing dialogue time together bonded the Council members in a new and different way. Learning to listen to each other generated a higher level of respect and awareness of their interdependence. It was a profound event which touched their souls and left each of them better for having had the experience.

Throughout this book there have been examples about people using dialogue. Each situation occurred because a space was created for dialogue to emerge. We will share insights on how different approaches help or hinder the creation of this space. These methods were used to help us as novices to become comfortable with the ways of dialogue. It is important to realize that we do not want to structure the experience to the point where it is stifled. In its purest form, dialogue happens without structure or facilitation. These creative approaches are offered to help

us break our developed patterns of interaction and remember our primal roots of connecting in simpler, more genuine ways.

As mentioned previously, individuals can practice dialogue on their own in daily interactions. It is very exciting when an entire group or community can together establish a common ground on the principles and practices. The worksheet on pages 151-152 outlines a brief process for groups to use. The worksheet concisely summarizes the definition, purpose, guidelines, and flow of a dialogue interaction. It has been used by hundreds of people and has proven to be very helpful.

DIALOGUE INTROSPECTION
Dialogue is a process that enhances the emergence of truth.

What is Dialogue?

How is dialogue different from other forms of conversation?
  Debate - "To beat down."
  Deliberate - "To weigh out."
  Discussion - "To break apart."
Most of our meetings are like ping pong matches in which the participants bat their opinion around the room or like merging traffic in which there is little listening, just waiting for an opening to get one's opinion inserted. Discussion is not bad. It is often how we make decisions and get things done.

Dialogue: "A flow of meaning."
Dialogue is another form of conversation in which we genuinely inquire into ways of thinking that we take for granted. It is not about trying to come to consensus or make a decision, but rather to explore and reflect, to listen to everyone's thinking as just as valid as my own, to be willing to examine my own thinking and be influenced by the thinking of others.

Examples of distinctions between dialogue and discussion:

Discussion	Dialogue
Defend	Explore
Certainty	Uncertainty
Competence	Vulnerability
Know	Learn
Separation	Connection
Stating	Uncovering
Expert	Beginner
Opinion	Truth
Judging	Searching
Dependent/ Independent	Interdependent

Share some of these guidelines.

Guidelines for the emergence of dialogue:
a. Leave our roles and positions outside.
b. Display and genuinely questions our assumptions and those of others.
c. Suspend certainty and judgment.
d. Slow down, leave space between comments.
e. Have a willingness to be surprised and influenced by another.
f. Not here to fix, manage, or process.
g. No hidden agendas or perplexed outcomes.
h. Allow for silence.
i. Speak from "I" and listen to the "WE."
j. Allow multiple perspectives to surface without needing to resolve them.
k. Consider others' perspectives/opinions as just as valid as your own.

Thoughts, Realizations, Wonderings, Learnings
(FACILITATOR HINTS)
Note: This two page handout can be used by participants as a format to facilitate dialogue in their settings.

| **A Process for Dialogue to Emerge** | **Thoughts, Realizations, Wonderings, Learnings**
(FACILITATOR HINTS) |

1. Check-In.

A "Check In" is an invitation for each individual in the group to share his/her thinking. It is a way for other group members to practice listening skills and gain insights. Check-In sets the tone for being together in a different way.

2. Developing the Practice Field.

The purpose of the practice field is to establish an environment where the conditions are prime for dialogue to emerge. A place where participants can practice the art of dialogue. It is really a list of considerations for the group that addresses how they wish to be together.

Sample practice field:
a. Keep confidentiality.
b. Speak from "I."
c. Listen deeply to others and yourself.
d. No side conversations or interruptions.
e. No assuming--check each other for understanding.
f. No agendas, no leaders, no judgments.
g. Value each person's contribution.
Additions from group:

3. Dialogue Question, Statement, or Quote.

Facilitator will read the question, statement, or quote and offer a moment of silence for participants to reflect.

4. Dialogue Experience.

Invite anyone to begin speaking as they feel moved to do so.

5. Debrief on Dialogue Experience.
a. Participants to write key learnings on 3x5 card and give to facilitator.
b. Invite participants to share their experiences and learnings with the group.

6. Closing Poem.

Facilitator Hints column:

1. *There will be a question provided for each person to answer during Check-In.*

2. *Share purpose and examples. Ask for additions from the group. They can record them on their individual dialogue introspection sheets.*

3. *Starting the Dialogue. Before we begin, it might be helpful to realize that what we are about to engage in may feel awkward because the pace is different. Sometimes there are moments of silence which we are not used to in the fast pace of our regular meetings.*

4. *Introduce the Question. To stimulate our thinking for the dialogue I(we) would like to first share the following questions, give you time to reflect, and then provide an opportunity for you to share your thinking with the person next to you.*

5. *After hearing the question, take a few minutes to think about your own questions and thinking with regard to this issue. Think even deeper and ask yourself what is behind that thinking? The question is:*

6. *As facilitator, feel free to share any realizations, observations, energies, and/or noticings you have about the dialogue experience.*

Thank everyone for participating. Note that speaking is not the sole indicator of participation. Many people participated by listening and experiencing internal dialogue, all of which are contributed to the experience and wisdom gained.

Dialogue is a time to practice relationship building skills of intention, listening, advocacy, inquiry, and silence

Considerations And Creative Approaches That Invite Dialogue

Time Frames And Location

Generally it takes some time for us to transition out of our fast paced lives into a slower space. We can experience dialogue anywhere, anytime, but it is helpful to plan it in a place where we will not be distracted, called away, or rushed. We have most commonly planned at least a two hour time frame, but have experienced longer and shorter times. Some have experienced dialogue in their work areas, but others have had to move elsewhere to avoid interruptions.

It is very distracting to have people leave the circle of discussion. The group feels a sense of loss. Someone in the dialogue should always acknowledge who is and who is not present. Some have said, if they must go away from the work site for two hours to experience dialogue, it will never happen. The response is, do what you can. In every situation where this issue has surfaced, and the group tried it anyway, they have not regretted it. Yes, we know it is not common practice for many, but this is part of changing some of what is commonplace in our work settings now.

Group Size, Diversity

We have experienced dialogue in groups from 10 to 150 people. There is not a set number for dialogue; however, there are considerations for smaller and larger groups. If the group is too small, it may be lacking in diversity. There may be limited insights because of the limited voices. Larger groups are more difficult because some feel intimidated to speak and it becomes difficult to hear. There have been times when we have divided a large group into smaller groups and then regretted not having them all together.

In spite of these concerns, dialogue has emerged as we embraced a spirit of experimentation and exploration. Try whatever the request, respond to the desires of others to engage in dialogue, and be trusting that what needs to emerge will emerge. It is important in any group for participants to be open and observant enough to notice what is blocking dialogue during this time together. It is amazing what groups can transcend once they are aware of what is presenting.

Room arrangement is a key consideration. The participants should be facing each other in a circle or oblong arrangement. The circle should be closed without gaps and no one should be sitting outside of the group. These considerations emphasize the spirit of inclusion and connectedness. For groups larger than 40 it has been helpful to have rows of seats with quarter circles facing the center.

Dialogue Facilitator Role

Dialogue does not necessarily need a facilitator, but in the beginning experiences, it has been very helpful. This is not a typical facilitator role. It is more the role of a learning guide and participant. As dialogue learning guides, we help create a safe open space for all to participate. We teach and practice the principles of dialogue. We observe the energy and interaction of the group and notice our own energy, feelings, and thoughts. It is not our place to judge the interaction or keep it on track. It is our role

to encourage curiosity and exploration. As learning guides, we ask participants to share their thinking behind their contributions and mirror back what we are noticing is occurring as the group proceeds. It is not our role to have the answers but to be a participant in the learning and uncovering of deeper issues with the group.

It is most important to be totally present as a facilitator, sending our energy and encouragement to each individual. We honor all voices equally and acknowledge when others are not honoring the voices. We do accept people where they are in their journey. It is sometimes difficult practicing patience when the dialogue is not moving forward. It is always best to delay when we feel the urge to intervene. In the worksheet presented on pages 151-152, there are examples of how the facilitator might intervene.

Practice Field Development

It does not matter if the dialogue participants know each other or are total strangers; a practice field is usually a good way to establish a common ground. A practice field is just as its name implies, a list of behaviors we wish to practice during this dialogue. It really represents how the group wants to be together. We have experimented with having the group develop one from scratch, or listing three or four commonly used items, and asking the group if they accept them or desire to add or change any of them. Either way has worked well. With a more novice group, it has been helpful to start with the common ones. The following are usually included in a sample practice field: keep confidentiality, speak from "I", listen deeply to others and yourself, no side conversations or interruptions, check each other for understanding, honor time, leave roles and positions outside, everyone is responsible for his/her own learning, celebrate diversity, and value each person's contribution.

Stimulating A Beginning

A good beginning is essential to creating the dialogue space. Most groups seem to appreciate a way to transition from thinking about their busy lives to being present in the moment. To encourage everyone to be centered, we usually use a Check-In process. The Check-In is an invitation for each individual in the group to share his/her thinking. It is a way for other participants to practice listening. It sets the tone for us to be together differently.

We have done Check-Ins with and without passing an object around for each person to hold while talking. Having an object is preferred. The object itself can evoke feelings and thinking. The object usually warms up as it is passed around the room connecting the energy of each individual. In one group we asked each of them to bring an item of personal significance with them and Check-In by saying why they brought it and what significance it held for them. At the conclusion, the participants knew more about each other and had developed connections.

An example of this type of Check-In is presented in the next Wisdom From The Field.

Wisdom From The Field

A room was packed with about 40 people at a one and a half hour session at a national health care conference entitled, "Leading From Body, Mind, and Spirit." My colleague, Jeanne, and I (Laurie Shiparski) were the facilitators and really had not planned this session as a dialogue but were incorporating the principles of dialogue and beginning with a Check-In. Often during Check-In an object is passed from one person to the next to remind us to listen to the voice that is speaking. The object passed was a piece of the Berlin Wall because the session was about building personal capacity during times of transition. The question was, "What have you learned about yourself in the midst of change and chaos?" This question evoked "I" statements from all in attendance.

As I began the Check-In I offered words from my heart, words of vulnerability and openness. It was my own vulnerability that extended the invitation for the rest of the group to feel comfortable doing the same. As each person spoke, there was an overwhelming energy in the room. A deep silence was felt in between those speaking.

The Check-In very quickly moved the group into dialogue. At this point we chose not to present our content. When this kind of genuine, collective wisdom emerges, we must be willing to go with it. One partici-

pant said she was going to leave in the beginning, but as soon as it got started she felt as though something was holding her feet to the ground--she could not leave. With each person's words came profound wisdom about resilience and the human spirit.

Some participants commented that they did not know why they had such feeling about the topic; they had no reasonable explanation for their emotion. It was as if the group moved from individual feeling to feeling the collective energy of the group. It was a life changing experience for us.

Afterwards everyone was tired, but did not want to leave. We had experienced something very special that day. Jeanne and I, who were experienced with dialogue, tried to understand why this had been such a great session in hopes of reproducing it. A wise colleague, Megan Bronson, offered a perspective on this dialogue that will not be forgotten. She said, "It does not matter what the question is, once the space is created, that which needs to emerge will emerge. That which needs to be given voice will come forth." She also said, "These experiences cannot be duplicated; each dialogue takes on its own life and each experience is what it needs to be for those present."

Music and art can also be used to begin. Each individual can offer what energy the music or art held for them. One very interesting method of Check-In has been to use lightstones. These are an array of stones that are hand painted with a picture on one side and a word representing a spiritual virtue on the other side. It has worked well to list the words on a flip chart or board and pass the stones around for each participant to choose the stone that attracts them and explain why to the other participants. Some of the words include courage, perseverance, respect, trust, unity, play, magic, joy, life, and transformation. The words seem to carry through the rest of the dialogue as people are reminded of them by the stones.

There are many questions or quotes that have been used to initiate dialogue. Sometimes it is as simple as, "What are you feeling as you come here today?" It is best to keep it simple. The best questions have been "I" questions which help us center on ourselves from the very beginning. Intriguing questions or quotes that evoked energy from dialogue participants include the following:

- What is one thing you have learned about yourself during change?
- "Each of us must be the change we want to see in the world," Ghandi.
- What aspect of your work holds purpose and meaning for you?
- What does it mean to bring your whole self to work?
- What have I learned about being a good partner?
- In what way have I changed over the past year as I have experienced change?
- In what way will I impact the destiny of nursing?
- What is the nature of equal worth in the work place?
- What has been my learning about relationships during chaos?
- What is the nature of _____. (i.e., change, vulnerability, humanism, growth, learning.)
- What is one thing I need to change in myself to become a better partner?

It is always important to offer a minute of silence after presenting the question for everyone to think about it. We usually remind people to release the worry of what they are going to say when it is their turn; it is more effective to speak from the heart at the moment of your turn. It is not uncommon for the Check-In to lead right into dialogue. Some of our most powerful dialogue experiences have begun with a Check-In.

In some environments, the Check-In, when introduced, became a target for mockery. As participants experience the insights and learning, they often change their minds. One benefit of a Check-In is the uncovering of feelings that individuals bring with them that have no connection with the meeting or dialogue. The other participants come to know the situation, and the proliferation of untrue assumptions is prevented. In the end, the quality of the dialogue has less to do with a question or quote, and more to do with noticing what needs to emerge.

Expanding The Dialogue Experience

We have covered the principles of dialogue throughout this book; intention, inquiry, advocacy, listening, and silence. Throughout the dialogue it is imperative to continually deepen the experience through

the use of these principles. This promotes an uncovering by removing the layers of our thinking. We are seeking the thinking behind our thinking and being.

Eventually, the experience takes on a collective consciousness that is maintained. We have experienced energy and feeling about issues that are not solely ours. It is almost like there is a dynamic feeling or voice that is swirling in the room looking for a human being from whom to emerge. This may sound too far out for some reading it, but you need only experience it once to realize it is an untapped field of potential and you will hunger for more.

Concluding Dialogue

The dialogue ends when we run out of time, or we sense the energy in the room decreasing. It is important to be respectful and honor time commitments. Someone usually notices and questions the group as to what they desire to do. In some situations, the option is there for a group to continue. In concluding, the facilitator can ask if anyone has the need to give voice to one last thought. It is a very good practice to take about ten minutes at the end to debrief on the experience. This has been especially helpful as we continue to learn and practice dialogue. We might ask, "How was this experience for you? What did you notice? How did it feel?"

As we surface key learning, we stimulate even more learning. It is again worth mentioning the value of capturing key learning as it relates to concluding dialogue. After having participants record their key learning on a 3x5 card we can ask them to share it out loud if there is time. Reviewing individual learning in this way has made visible the pearls of wisdom gained and has generated even more learning from the learning. It may even be helpful to ask the group if the key learning could be typed and shared with others. This is one way to get a sense of the outcomes of dialogue. Most key learning has been very impressive as it reveals a level of personal learning rarely experienced in more traditional learning experiences.

A "Check-Out" can also be considered using either a brief or long process. As mentioned, key learning can be verbally shared. We have also used a quick question such as, "Say one word that describes how you are feeling now." This Check-Out helps to bring closure to the dialogue so that everyone leaves feeling connected. What more appropriate way to conclude than hearing each person's voice one more time? In addition, sometimes a poem, reading, or quote can be read to conclude.

Fred Kofman (1994) has written a concise article regarding Check-Ins and Check-Outs. He shares with us that the Native American people called Check-In and Check-Out "Council Rounds." They followed the simple rule to be brief, and speak from the heart. How would our meetings be different if we used the Check-In and Check-Out process?

What are some of the barriers to dialogue? As we proceed in bringing the experience of dialogue into our lives, it behooves us to consider a few of the barriers that are commonly encountered. In our work cultures today, the presence of competition has been a major barrier to us communicating with and trusting each other. The tide is turning away from competition in many places as they learn that connections with others offer abundant possibilities where competition was limiting.

The poem on page 168 offers thinking around competition. There is not a place for competition in dialogue, and we are summoned to find ways to transcend it.

Other barriers include:

- Being impatient with ourselves and others as we experiment.

- Past institutional and hierarchical patterns.

- Not fully embracing the principles of dialogue.

- Selective attention.

- Defending views.

- Listening to judge.

- Failing to explore assumptions.

- Trying to force dialogue to happen.

As we participate in dialogue, we can be aware of these barriers to avoid or address as they arise.

A Community Of Competition

Some say motivation and progress
reign in a community of competition.
That it breeds the best for all
and helps us fulfill a vision.

But there is another side
to this community of gold,
it's dark shadow noticed
we may not wish to hold.

With competition also comes
an insatiable, gnawing thirst.
One that drives the best of us
to selfishly prove we're first.

It becomes a game to win
and ego must take all,
pitting people against people
the outcome anyone's call.

Relationships do suffer
as the casualties of fight,
we make each other look bad
just to give ourselves more height.

The victims at the heart of this
are those we seek to serve.
They get caught in the crossfire
missing out on care deserved.

So in the end the very thing
that promised us success,
divides us from each other
where collective power manifests.

- Laurie Shiparski

How do we know when we have done it? This is a most common question from those who are beginning to learn dialogue. It is difficult to describe at what point discussion crosses the threshold to dialogue. The following poem offers insights on this issue.

Dialogue: Have We Done It?

Dialogue; how do we know
when we've done it?

When our ears hear for the first time
the true voices of our colleagues.

When our eyes see for the first time
each person as a reflection of all humanity.

When our mouths speak for the first time
genuine words from the heart.

When our bodies feel for the first time
the individual and collective energy of life.

When our minds meet for the first time
and universal truths are uncovered.

When our spirits meet for the first time
and we realize the power
of something greater than ourselves.

- Laurie Shiparski

The poem on page 169 was inspired by one who has experienced dialogue. It is an experience that is difficult to put into words. It is not that we have not experienced these things before in life; in dialogue it feels like the first time, every time. We have also noticed that it has an effect on us that stays with us after the actual experience. Each time we engage in it, another layer of understanding is revealed and our thinking and being is altered forever.

Is dialogue always a beautiful, calm experience? Absolutely not. As discussed earlier, a desired event in dialogue is to welcome diversity, polarity, and disagreement. We have been in dialogues where extreme human pain emerges or harsh disagreements surface. It has also happened where groups have uncovered a deeper issue by which they are troubled and will have to face now that it is out in the open--the difference being as these issues surface in dialogue, we react differently than before. We are open to what is being brought and do not become defensive. We are seeking understanding, not necessarily the right answer. An example of this instance is revealed in this Wisdom From The Field.

Wisdom From The field

A diverse group of about 25 from a hospital gathered for a dialogue. They were undergoing great change in redesign and restructuring. They were progressive, caring people committed to their mission of serving their community. In their culture was hierarchy, and they wanted more insights on why this persisted even when they were trying to shift out of it. The dialogue question was, *What is the nature of equal worth in the work place?* We started with a practice field and Check-In using this question. As each voice contributed, the picture emerged.

Immediately following the Check-In, the questions came and there was discomfort in the room. The views that surfaced were divergent and opposing. Some in the room realized they did not actually believe that each human had the same worth.

We realized there was a hierarchy because many of us in the room were perpetuating it. There were beliefs that physicians were the only care givers who offered healing services to patients versus beliefs that everyone from the physician to the housekeeper offered such care. Beliefs

emerged from some who judged patients who were homeless, prostitutes, or elderly as less worthy of care versus those who believed every human life is as worthy as the next.

It was very tense as these opposing views emerged. Some said they had not even realized they had these views while others could not believe their colleagues had such opposing views. It was clear to the group why their daily work felt difficult.

We all had to focus our listening and check our internal dialogues as the passionate words swirled in the room. At the conclusion of our time there had been many issues uncovered. There was relief in knowing the deeper issues, yet a heavy realization of the work ahead. We were sure of one thing: we were all in this together and there was a collective commitment to keeping this dialogue open as we learned and grew together.

It is necessary to comment on one last aspect of "Have we done it?" Some of us at one time or another have been so preoccupied with deciding if we are experiencing dialogue or not that we actually blocked its emergence. We have to let this fixation go.

The risk is to make dialogue a difficult thing to achieve. We have to resist the temptation to make it mechanical. We must relax and be content with whatever happens; this is the nature of dialogue. Sometimes we are surprised when a group immediately goes deep into dialogue and wonder how this happened. Other times, all conditions seem prime and we get stuck in discussion.

One thing is for certain, dialogue cannot be predicted, controlled, forced, or measured. We have to acknowledge and develop comfort with its nature. We already have comfort levels with other unexplainable events in life and accept them as miracles and mystery. Dialogue is a genuine human experience, and we will know when we are engaged in it.

Dialogue provides sustenance for the future. Dialogue is important to us personally and organizationally as we move into the next millennium. Dialogue can help us to connect and radically change the way we work together. Have we forgotten our responsibility to co-create today for a better tomorrow? Many of our present values, perceptions, and practices in the work place are changing. Dialogue will continue to evolve and offer hope for us to find ways to nourish ourselves, our work communities, and our society at large. We must be ready when the hungry call for more dialogue.

Loaves And Fishes

This is not
the age of information

This is *not*
the age of information.

Forget the news,
and the radio,
and the blurred screen.

This is the time
of loaves
and fishes.

People are hungry,
and one good word is bread
for a thousand.

- David Whyte

CLOSING THOUGHTS

Every human being has a great,
yet often unknown, gift to care,
to be compassionate,
to become present to the other,
to listen, to hear and receive.
If that gift would be set free
and made available,
miracles could take place.
- Henri J. M. Nouwen

$\mathcal{D}$ialogue creates a space that sets free the gift which Nouwen (1974) describes. Over the last 14 years of intimate work with multiple clinical settings, the patterns are the same. There is a call, maybe best described as a plea for help, to humanize the work setting. Human beings thrive in a culture where there is shared purpose, continuous learning, expanded thinking, and healthy relationships. There is nothing more stimulating than sharing meaningful work with others. Dialogue connects people through shared meaning. It is an invitation to experience miracles in the work place.

The legacy of this generation of humans will be that we created a health care system, a true health system that will extend into the homes, the work settings, the universe. It will look nothing like what we know today. It will be nothing like the present narrow mindset that confines the concept of health within the halls of hospitals or medical clinics or within the narrow accountabilities of one health care professional over another, or the fight for control, money, and power. In the new health care system, there will be a network of people who come to work every day with the intention of helping maintain the balance of BodyMindSpirit. They will be the health care providers.

The shift is happening. The evidence is the chaos that exists in the health care system. It has opened the possibilities to transcend the present realities. The initial work to form a network of people to serve this humanity is occurring everywhere. It is evident in the mergers of medical care settings across the continent. Or is it? Without dialogue we will get lost in the task and the doing but not the purpose. For example, mergers will be take-overs, not networking.

If there is no conscious intention to make sure that the work is linked to the essence of our humanity, we will create a system that will further disconnect us as human beings.

We know the alternative to dialogue. We see it every day in our work. We see, for example, mergers driven by bottom line, greed and "power-over." We know what happens when the Body, Mind, and Spirit are not linked. When not linked, actions are driven by the narrow focus of the body to do everything to survive, and the mind to take control and power. The result is decision making that never goes to the deeper wisdom of the Soul, the core of humanness. Without the input of the love and compassion that sits in the Soul, the very goal we hope to achieve as humans is blocked within the empty promises of a disconnected Body and Mind. Life, the meaningful purpose, is lost once again in the doing, not in "becoming." The sick cycle of destruction of the human being continues. Dialogue links the BodyMindSpirit and stops the cycle.

There can be no dialogue if people do not have the time to be together. As obvious as it might seem, it is not happening in the work setting. Dialogue requires that people be together, not just to do, but to become. Becoming is a desire that sits in the Soul of each human being. The people surrounded by the flurry and chaos of the day are constantly asking the same question, *How do we do it?* Creating an infrastructure to make that happen has been the core of our work at the CPM Resource Center. It is the process to assure that people are linked so they can dialogue and continue their important work. How to do it, the logistics of assuring the time and place to connect, is the purpose of our next book and video series. See Appendix.

We have come to know the hope that rests in living dialogue. There is no utopia; there is only the work to continuously honor the wholeness of our being and integrate it into the fiber of our lives. Dialogue is a strategy that has proven itself over time. It is an old and ancient behavior of the human being. It is an approach that has evolved out of the core of our humanness. It offers us endless possibilities that emerge from a peaceful place within the Souls of a connected humanity. It is not a quick fix; it is a commitment to never lose site of our accountability "to learn to live as human beings." It is not enough to talk about freeing the Spirit, we must first talk with one another so we can free it and tap our human capacity. We hope this book will help you bring dialogue into your life, and into your work setting. *It is the living of dialogue, not the reading, thinking, or discussion of it that is most important. It is the end of this book where the real beginning takes place.*

BIBLIOGRAPHY

Gunn Allen, P. (1991). Words and Language: A Haggle. Sewell, M. (Ed.), <u>Cries of the spirit</u>. (p. 285). Boston, MA: Beacon Press.

Anderson, D. (1995). <u>Act now</u>. Minneapolis: Chronimed Publishing.

Bohm, D. (1989). <u>On dialogue</u>. Ojai, CA: David Bohm Seminars.

Brown, J. (1996). <u>The choice</u>. Berkeley: Conari Press.

Brown, J. <u>Choosing</u>. Unpublished. Used with author's permission.

Campbell, J. and Moyers, B. (1988). <u>The power of myth</u>. New York: Doubleday.

Fox, E. (1941). <u>Find and use your inner power</u>. San Francisco: Harper Collins Publisher.

Havel, V. (1990, February). Address to a Joint Session of the United States Congress, Washington, DC.

Isaacs, W. (April, 1993). "Dialogue: The power of collective thinking." The Systems Thinker, 4(3), p. 1-5.

Jandernoa, B. (October, 1995). <u>Dialogue: Thinking, learning, and creating together</u>. Presented at the CPM National Conference, Phoenix, AZ.

Jones, M. (1995). <u>Creating an imaginative life</u>. Berkeley: Conari Press.

Kabat-Zinn, J. (1994). <u>Wherever you go, there you are</u>. New York: Hyperion.

Kofman, F. (1994). "Check-in, check-out: A tool for 'real' conversations." The Systems Thinker, 5(4), p. 8-9.

Kriegel, R. and Brandt, D. (1996). Sacred cows make the best burgers. New York: Warner Books.

Krishnamurti, J. (1992). On relationship. New York: Harper Collins Publishers.

Kritek, P. (1996). Negotiating at an uneven table. San Francisco: Jossey-Bass Publishers.

Merton, T. (1961). New seeds of contemplation. New York: New Directions Publishing.

Myss, C. (1994). Why people don't heal. (Cassette Recording No. 1-56455-310-8). Boulder, CO: Sounds True.

Nouwen, H. (1974). Out of solitude. Notre Dame, IN: Ave Maria Press.

Nouwen, H. (1981). The way of the heart. New York: Ballantine Books.

Palmer, Parker, J. Leading from within. Reflections on spirituality and leadership. Indianapolis, IN: Campus Ministries. (Available from Potter's House Book Service, 1658 Columbia Road NW, Washington, DC, 20009.)

Remen, R. N. (1996). Kitchen table wisdom. New York: Riverhead Book.

Senge, P., Roberts, C., Ross, R., Smith, B., and Kleiner, A. (1994). The fifth discipline fieldbook. New York: Currency Doubleday.

Shiparski, L. (1997). Change is life: Poems of personal transformation in the work place. Michigan: Practice Field Publishing.

Theresa, Mother. (1996). Meditations from a simple path. New York: Ballantine Books.

Underwood, P. (October, 1996). Learning your way through chaos: Balance in the midst of change. Presented at the CPM National Conference, Grand Rapids, MI.

Wesorick, B. (1995). <u>The closing and opening of a millennium: A journey from old to new thinking</u>. Michigan: Practice Field Publishing.

Wesorick, B. (1996). <u>The closing and opening of a millennium: A journey from old to new relationships in the work setting</u>. Michigan: Practice Field Publishing.

Wheatley, M., Kellner-Rogers, M. (1996). <u>A simpler way</u>. San Francisco, CA: Berrett-Koehler Publishers, Inc.

Whyte, D. (1994). <u>The heart aroused</u>. New York: Currency Doubleday.

Whyte, D. (1997). <u>The house of belonging</u>. Langley, WA: Many Rivers Press.

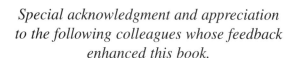

*Special acknowledgment and appreciation
to the following colleagues whose feedback
enhanced this book.*

Betty Jo Balzar	Ken Miller
Linda Barnes	Jim Moore
Margie Bosscher	Pat Nakoneczny
Mike Bosscher	Tim Porter-O'Grady
Margaret Bowles	Jeanne Roode
Judy Brown	Mary Kay Russell
Margret Comack	Barb Scarpelli
Carol Glass	Cathy Schwartz
Mary Gray	Chris Shaw
Karen Grigsby	Mike Shiparski
Ellen Hale	Rani Srivastava
Carmen Hall	Brenda Srof
Shirley Hamann	Ellen Stuart
Diane Hanson	Paula Underwood
Rochelle Jee	Diane Uustal
Darlene Josephs	Marcia Veenstra
Mary Koloroutis	Judie Walker
Connie McAllister	Donna Westmoreland
Katherine McIndoe	Kathy Wyngarden

*A special thank you to Linda DeLeeuw
who coordinated this entire effort including
typing and manuscript layout.*

APPENDIX

Clinical Practice Model
Resource Center (CPMRC)
Grand Rapids, Michigan

<u>Mission:</u>
Enhance partnering relationships and world linkages for generation of collective knowledge and wisdom that continually improves the structure, process and outcomes of professional service and community health.

Bonnie Wesorick, RN, MSN
Founder

Laurie Shiparski, RN, BSN, MS
Professional Practice Specialist

Diane Hanson, RN, BSN, MM
Practice Guidelines Specialist

Ellen Hale, RN, MSN
Informatics Specialist

Darlene Josephs, CPS
Operations Administrator

Linda DeLeeuw
Administrative Secretary

Marie Kegel
Administrative Secretary

Researchers:
Karen Grigsby, RN, PhD
Donna Westmoreland, RN, PhD
University of Nebraska Medical Center
College of Nursing, Omaha, NE

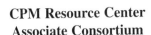

CPM Resource Center
Associate Consortium

Mission:

Collectively create professional practice and learning environments that empower each partner to provide their unique healing contribution.

Linda Engdahl, RN, MS
Mary Koloroutis, RN, MS
Abbott Northwestern
Hospital
Minneapolis, MN

Betty Jo Balzar, RN, MSN
Appleton Medical Center
Appleton, WI

Michelle Troseth, RN, BSN
Bonnie Wesorick, RN, MSN
Senior Advisor for
Professional Practice
Kathy Wyngarden, RN,
MSN
Butterworth Hospital
Grand Rapids, MI

Dee Blakey, RN, BSN
Flagstaff Medical Center
Flagstaff, AZ

Brenda Srof, RN, MSN
Goshen College
Goshen, IN

Diane Thomas, RN, MSN,
CETN
Harris Continued Care
Hospital
Bedford, TX

Marilyn Knight, RN, MSN
Harris Home Health
Fort Worth, TX

Kathy Ratliff, RN, ADN
Harris Methodist Erath
Stephenville, TX

Nancy Pittman, RN, MS, CNA
Harris Methodist Fort
Worth
Forth Worth, TX

Kelly Smith, RN, RN
Harris Methodist - HEB
Hospital
Bedford, TX

Rochelle Jee, RN, BSN
Harris Methodist
Southwest/Northwest
Fort Worth, TX

Markeeta Edwards, RN, BSN
Harris Methodist - Walls
Regional
Cleburne, TX

Marsha Vanderveen, RNC,
MS
Holland Community
Hospital
Holland, MI

Home Health Care
Holland, MI

*Barbara Scarpelli, RN,
BScN*
Hotel Dieu Grace Hospital
Windsor, Ontario, Canada

Linda Dietrich, RN, MSN
Kaiser Sunnyside Hospital
Clackamas, OR

Liberty Hospital
Liberty, MO

*Karen Kline, RN, MScN
Katherine McIndoe, RN,
MSN*
Lions Gate Hospital
North Vancouver, British
Columbia, Canada

Elaine Keller
Macomb Hospital Center
Warren, MI

Linda Barnes, RN, BS
Magic Valley Regional
Medical Center
Twin Falls, ID

*Shirley Hamann, RN,
MSN, ONC*
Medcenter One
Bismarck, ND

Cathy Schwartz, RN, MS
Memorial Medical Center
Springfield, IL

Cindy Kallsen, RN, BSN
Mercy Hospital
Council Bluffs, IA

Pat Nakoneczny, RN, BSN
Northern Michigan
Hospital
Petoskey, MI

Debra Skidmore, RN, BSN
Phoenix Children's
Hospital
Phoenix, AZ

Glenda Skaggs, RN, BSN
St. Catherine Hospital
Garden City, KS

Saint Joseph Health Center
Kansas City, MO

*Deb Zielinski, RN, BSN,
CCRN*
St. Jude Medical Center
Fullerton, CA

*Sue Chase-Cantarini, RN,
MS*
St. Mark's Hospital
Salt Lake City, UT

Mary Gray, RN, MSN
St. Mary-Corwin Regional
Medical Center
Pueblo, CO

Betty Jo Balzar, RN, MSN
Theda Clark Medical
Center
Neenah, WI

*Margret Comack, BN,
MEd*
Toronto East General
Hospital
Toronto, Ontario, Canada

Lanyce Keel,
University of Nebraska
Medical Center
Omaha, NE

Laurie Egeland, RNC, BSN
Visiting Nurse Services
Grand Rapids, MI

Mary Grondin, RN, BScN
Shari Jones, RN, BScN
Marilyn Smillie, RN, BScN
Rani Srivastava, RN, MScN
Wellesley Central Hospital
Toronto, Ontario, Canada

Chrystle Whitaker, RN
Wesley Medical Center
Wichita, KS

Chris Shaw, RN, BSN
West Allis Memorial Hospital
West Allis, WI

Send any comments or inquiries regarding this journey to:

CPM Resource Center
100 Michigan Street NE
Grand Rapids, MI 49503
616/391-2017
616/391-2770 FAX
ldeleeuw.@bw.brhn.org

"Thoughts"

Additional Resources

Books:

Wisdom From The Field Series:

The Closing And Opening Of A Millennium: A Journey From Old To New Thinking, Book I – Bonnie Wesorick

The Closing And Opening Of A Millennium: A Journey From Old To New Relationships In The Work Setting, Book II – Bonnie Wesorick

Change Is Life: Poems Of Personal Transformation In The Work Place – Laurie Shiparski

Audio Cassettes:

A Place Within – Diane Penning

Celebration Of Life: A Dedication To Nurses

Diane Penning: A Personal Christmas

Video Series:

The Partnership Council Video and Field Book, along with other teaching/learning resources from the Wisdom From The Field Video Series, can be obtained by contacting the CPM Resource Center:

CPM Resource Center
100 Michigan Street NE
Grand Rapids, MI 49503
616/391-2017
ldeleeuw@bw.brhn.org